TROUBLE PROOFING KIDS
3rd Edition

*A program for parents
interested in teaching
their children and adolescents
how to stay out of trouble forever,
and
to help them be proud for doing so!*

By

Tom Gnagey

Clinical Psychologist, Educator

© 2013, 2019

The Family of Man Press

1

2

Chapter One

John and Bob are both fourteen and both are known to me personally as real youngsters. They live on the same street, both are the second child in a family of four children and are of the same race and religion. Both live with their natural mother and father and their homes would be classified as lower middle class in terms of income and lifestyle. Both boys are freshmen at the same high school, and both are enrolled in a general studies program - academically, one step up the ladder from a straight trade school program and one down from college prep. Both are average to slightly above average in general intelligence and both have average ability to win friends and influence people.

John has never had so much as a close encounter with the police and has seldom had to engage in fights or other social conflicts. His school conduct is outstanding. He is liked by teachers and students, alike. He and his family really enjoy each other - this is not to say they don't have those normal disagreements. John has had his share of grounding and other corrective steps, but he seldom fails to learn his lesson the first time.

Bob has been in trouble with the law since he was eight, has twice been engaged in brutal beatings of other youngsters and has stolen things so often he couldn't begin to tell you which of his possessions are really his and which have been pilfered. Reportedly, he is already the father of three children. He holds the school record for number of hours assigned to detention, though he seldom shows up to serve them. He both sells and uses whatever drugs are available at the moment. Last month he was hospitalized with a broken nose, a dislocated shoulder, and four broken ribs, after being attacked by a group of boys in the locker room, at school.

Two boys from very similar backgrounds and social settings, and yet one has somehow become remarkably trouble-proofed and the other, forever trouble-prone. How could this happen? What things make the difference? How can, and do, families, neighborhoods, schools, and other agencies contribute one way or the other? What do they do or not do that predispose children to become either trouble-proofed or trouble-prone? Is there some kind of mystical formula or magical potion that makes the difference? Is it just a matter of chance or luck?

What is Trouble-Proofing?

In no way is it a matter of chance or luck. The reasons some youngsters grow into trouble-proofed human beings and others do not, is absolutely no mystery, whatsoever. There is a formula - an almost foolproof formula. To those who don't understand these well-established methods, it may, in fact, seem like a magic potion or a matter of chance, but to those who do understand, success is just a matter of dedicated attention to the proper details, and some hard, carefully planned, wonderfully rewarding, work.

The secret is not where one lives or what one's color or ethnic background happens to be. It is not whether a child lives with one or both parents, or is the first, second or twentieth child in the family. It is not whether the family is poor or rich or somewhere in between. It is not a matter of attending or not attending religious services every week (though in some cases the values learned there may help). It is not a matter of being highly educated or less educated.

The secret is primarily a matter of the philosophy of life the child learns (almost always at home) and accepts as his own. (The term primarily suggests some exceptions, and I will deal with them later on. Until then, go ahead and think of trouble-proofing as basically a matter of philosophy - that is, a matter of the beliefs – values – he holds about life and how it should be lived.)

All of what I will be presenting here is reasonably founded in many reliable, scientific studies of human behavior and in the best common sense and wisdom from both the most successful parents and the greatest thinkers about such matters down through the course of human history. Having used this approach myself with many, many hundreds of children and families, representing almost every conceivable set of circumstances and belief systems, I can assure you that it works. In fact, when properly applied throughout, it virtually always works.

In a nutshell here is the thesis, the core, the basic propositions of this program:

Help the child learn and accept the positive assumption that, under virtually all circumstances, each human being has a significant and lasting responsibility for the welfare, safety, success and happiness of all other human beings (including that child, himself), and you will absolutely fashion a trouble-proofed kid, forever

Let me say it one more time a bit more simply: Help the child believe that every human being has a real, lifelong responsibility to keep all people safe, happy, comfortable, and successful, and you will have built a strong and confident, trouble-proofed kid, forever.

This formula is just that simple. Most other formulas seem to fail. Making this one work requires a measure of specialized knowledge and the careful application of several proven procedures. It also requires the acceptance of some very basic, easy to understand, philosophic principles - I call them values or tenets. These values are compatible with almost all other positive belief systems, whether by nature they are part of a given religion, are nonsectarian, are humanistic or are otherwise constructed. The only doctrines that seem totally incompatible with trouble-proofing are those that preach hate toward some other group of human beings or that teach we are each basically bad, undeserving beings.

What is the purpose of this program?

It is the purpose of this program to present:

First: Those several important philosophic tenets (values);

Second: The necessary basic knowledge gleaned from science, common sense, and effective parenting;

Third: A set of necessary priorities; and

Fourth: The specific procedures that can then be used to build trouble-proofed kids.

If you are merely participating, here, in order to gain a basic understanding of this approach, by all means skim along at whatever pace feels comfortable. If, however, you are a parent or a child welfare practitioner, or if you are an adolescent hoping to find some answers for yourself, or are anyone else wanting to master the techniques presented in this program, I urge you to pay very close attention to each and every step. Complete every paragraph and every assignment when it occurs and complete it exactly as outlined in the program. Otherwise, this approach will have a significantly reduced chance of success for you. To go back and clarify the concepts or do the assignments later on, defeats a major strength of the carefully planned sequencing built into this program. Once skipped, an idea or an assignment may never again provide you with its full effect, because its impact will have been diluted or redefined by what has followed.

Those who are familiar with some of my other programs or audio books will recognize the repetitive basic tenets - those known collectively as a philosophy of life which I call, Reciprocal

Esteem - in this case re-applied specifically to the task of trouble-proofing kids.

There are so many kinds of troubles that can befall our children today. We see them turning away from education; becoming violent people; refusing to live according to the law; making harmful friendship choices; giving up on themselves and/or on life; searching for the good life along such artificial and dangerous avenues as drugs, alcohol and tobacco, gangs, dropping out of school, thieving, bullying, engaging in ill-timed or dangerous sexual activity; premature parenthood; affiliating with hate groups or philosophies; failing to develop the essential ability to delay gratification; 'machoism'; identity problems stemming from not having a same-sex, same-race, adult role model in the home or readily available; problems that seem to grow out of financial limitations; and on down a long and all too familiar list. The menu of possible troubles just seems endless, these days. Since it is unlikely that we can teach children specifically how to avoid each and every one of these many individual and ever-present pitfalls, how can we proceed?

Trouble-proofing kids presents a tried and proven philosophy and set of techniques aimed at helping youngsters make those decisions that will protect themselves from becoming involved in such troublesome ways of life. Its premise is, that although we can never protect children from having to face the problems and temptations that will invariably confront them, we can teach them how to sense potentially troublesome and dangerous situations and ideas, to effectively analyze them for their probable outcomes before taking action, and to make appropriate decisions that will keep them from embracing or falling prey to the troubles those situations produce or allow.

Approaches to controlling behavior

Societies in general, social agencies, schools, and families, typically use one or more of the three basic approaches to controlling behavior. One is the punishment approach in which offenders are hurt in some way for their misbehavior (that is, behavior that is not in accord with the boss's rules and expectations). 'Bad' behavior is punished, and 'good' behavior, since it is just expected, is most often, ignored. This approach is based on the assumption that, either (1) we will always be caught when we misbehave (so we can then be punished), or (2) that we will be made so fearful of the possible pain of punishment, that we will just mindlessly behave according to the boss's rules, in order to avoid ever being hurt.

The second behavior control method is the reward approach in which we are recognized in positive, rewarding, pleasurable ways for our appropriate or acceptable behavior (behavior that is, again, acceptable to someone else who is in charge of us, and not necessarily to us). Good behavior is rewarded, and bad behavior is ignored, the belief being that if it is not rewarded it will stop occurring. Again, the approach relies on the assumption that either (1) we will be seen behaving appropriately by someone with the authority to administer the reward, or (2) that the act of being a good guy (as defined by that somebody else who is in charge of us) will just become natural, once we have received a sufficient, mind-altering, diet of randomly, though precisely dispensed, rewards.

In both of these first two behavior control methods, one person's behavior is controlled by a second, stronger, person's concept of what is desirable and or right.

The third approach to controlling behavior is what could be referred to as the acceptance of a set of inner positive values - my version of which I call Reciprocal Esteem. Whereas, punishment requires the presence of an external punisher or the threat of external punishment so severe that no one will ever risk misbehaving; and reward, requires the presence of an external force, in this case the external rewarder or the likelihood of a reward for the person; the Inner Positive Value approach derives its power, instead, primarily from inside the person, (kid) himself. Motivation to act appropriately or "right" depends on the belief or philosophy held by the person. It is a thoughtful, deliberate act, and not merely a response to a reward or punishment from someone else. People practicing this approach would say, "I do the right thing because I believe it is the right thing to do."

Now, we all act on what we believe is right, except when external rewards or punishments are great enough to make us deviate from those beliefs. Some people's beliefs are so weak or so unclear to them, that they are easily influenced by such outside forces as rewards or punishments. Some folks only value that which gets them what they want, right now, regardless of how it may affect anyone else (or even themselves, in the future). They will wait until the punisher is gone and then take what they want. The rewarder has no real lasting influence on this kind of person unless the reward happens to be something the person wants in the first place. If so, he'll do what is necessary to earn it if that doesn't entail more work than it would take to obtain the same thing some other way (like just stealing it).

Some will argue that we only learn to value that which keeps us from being punished or that which will likely result in a reward. The first argument comes, of course, from that camp, which believes in the use of punishment (pain and fear) as the best means of shaping the behavior of others, especially the behavior of those who tend to misbehave. The second comes from those promoting rewards. Since either or neither may or may not hold some validity, depending upon the circumstances, I choose to let those camps fight it out among themselves.

In the meantime, and quite pragmatically, I proceed according to what obviously works over the long haul of a lifetime - regardless of why it works. I call it Reciprocal Esteem. It is a positive value approach in which each individual person, using his or her own intellectual and emotional resources, decides that it makes the best all-around sense, for now and forevermore, to respect and support the broad span of other human beings' rights to be comfortable, safe, productive, happy, and self-fulfilled. I will continue to define and explain this philosophy - this way of believing - as we proceed.

How do we become who and what we are?

As we begin our quest to determine just how to go about

trouble-proofing our children, it seems essential for us to have a common basic pool of knowledge about how human beings grow to become themselves. Apparently, this has never been any big secret to thoughtful men, because we even find the several, now well-founded, fundamental principles, recorded many thousands of years ago in the earliest of mankind's written records. In general, we can fit all of these forces or operations into four main principles or categories. I will list them before going into a more detailed explanation.

First: The inborn and acquired physical and mental abilities and limitations each of us possess.

Second: The experiences and circumstances we have each met and endured as we have grown and matured.

Third: The quality of the human relationships we have experienced and used as the model for our own beliefs, values, and behaviors. And

Four: The type and intensity of that still mysterious inner spark that drives each individual along his or her particular path. Some call it motivation. Some think of it as spirit. Others speak of determination, disposition, or tenacity. By whatever name, it is that inner spark that drives us along our own particular path.

Let's take just a few minutes now to examine each of these four general categories in a bit more detail

Just as we all come into the World with a certain eye color and complexion tone, we also all come into the World with a given set of basic, built-in, possibilities. Regardless of the quality of those possibilities, some people live up to them - do as well as those abilities or limitations will allow - while others don't even come close.

For example, some people have the inborn potential for a strong, well-coordinated, athletically inclined body, while others have only some lesser degree of physical potential. Some are born with superior intellectual abilities and others with less. Some seem to be put together with a particular chemical make-up that predisposes them toward being either calm or active, easy-going or driven, organized or disorganized, attentive or distractible, patient or high-strung, and so on. Some folks are born with more skill when it comes to learning and thinking and being creative than are others. These inborn traits all represent the upper limits of possible achievement - those points that none of us can go beyond - although for one reason or another, many never come close to approaching their own particular level of potential.

In addition to the limits that our condition at birth sets for us, things may also go wrong, so to speak, as we grow up. Diseases and accidents may influence the way our bodies or brains are able to work. Certain kinds of experiences may affect us emotionally so that we are more able or less able to fully achieve our potential as well adjusted, loving, helpful human beings. The use of alcohol, tobacco, and other harmful drugs typically damages or at least diminishes certain physical, intellectual, and/or emotional capacities. Poor diet, inadequate exercise, and inconsistent sleep habits always take a toll on both body and mind.

So, we see that the raw human material we possess, as an infant, coupled with the effects of certain forces of man and nature, work together to set upper limits for our potential achievement levels. Aside from those "pre-set" physical and mental limitations - about which we can do very little - there are many other factors well within our own control and the control of those involved in the processes of raising us.

The experiences and circumstances with which we live, day-in and day-out, have a profound influence on who we are and who we become. For example, when our personal safety has to be a major concern and fear every day - as it is for the children in many of the violent city neighborhoods in the World today and in all abusive homes regardless of the neighborhood - a life is bent or twisted in a certain fearful or cautious way. Isn't it? Survival and vigilance become top priorities, and even after moving into safe havens those dangerous, fear-for-your-very-life times, may continue to affect one for the rest of his life.

Variations in the plain and simple physical circumstances of ones living conditions and how well they do, or do not, meet a child's basic needs for adequate shelter, safety, nourishment, clothing, cleanliness, physical care, predictable daily routine, and the like, will always have lasting and, either, helpful or haunting influences on one.

Few aspects of life affect us so deeply and thoroughly as the quality of our relationships with other human beings. It is largely through modeling those around us that we become who we eventually grow to be as a person. These early models, ultimately help shape the style of thinking we adopt, the way we define our emotional reactions, the behaviors we accept and reject in ourselves and others, the expectations we set for ourselves and have about others, the values and philosophy of life that we develop, and the other types of goals and over-all level of motivation that we set for ourselves.

The ways others treat us help define what kind of person we eventually come to believe we are - good or bad, likeable or not likeable, trustworthy or deceptive, accepting or rejecting, loving or hating, determined or submissive, capable or incompetent, and so on. Once we have figured out what kind of a person these influential people in our life think we are, we then often just go about living our life according to those judgments and perceptions. It is often as if we try to live up to their predictions for us.

Let's re-examine the circumstances and some of the experiences of the two boys I described at the beginning of this chapter. Remember John and Bob, the two fourteen-year-olds from the same neighborhood. As you will recall, John was becoming a capable, reliable, likeable, and successful human being, while Bob was already an irritating and utterly destructive thorn in the side of society.

In a moment, I will describe two home environments, and I want you to determine which one probably produced each young man. This exercise should prove two things. First, that you already know a great deal about what it takes to raise a trouble-proofed child. Second, that Bob was produced by a really lousy home that was based on ignorance of appropriate child raising-techniques, and John, by a really great and thoughtful home.

The Smiths were lower middle class. Mom worked as a house cleaner during the day and Dad as a night-shift mechanic.

Their combined income was about four hundred dollars a week (1991). The mother had graduated from high school and the father had eventually achieved his GED and then a trade school diploma. The Smith's home was filled with books and magazines and was the gathering place for the children's friends. Either the mother or the father was always present in the house when the children were there. The neighborhood children liked both of the adult Smiths. Mrs. Smith was every kids' listening post and Mr. Smith took them camping and had formed and coached the neighborhood's private version of three little league baseball teams. The rules in the Smith home were strict but fair and always enforced. Problems were talked out immediately and solutions were readily found to most conflicts. When solutions could not be agreed upon, the parent's decision prevailed. Homework always came before TV and most other activities. Each family member, including the six-year-old, was expected to engage in some kind of volunteer or charitable work each week. When you walked in the front door on Saturday morning you smelled fresh baked bread or cookies or oatmeal; and were met with lingering hugs from the smiling children and a warm handshake from Dad and Mom. The beds were made, the floors were clean, and all family members spoke respectfully with and about one another. There was always laughter, humor, smiles, and a helpful attitude. Well, need I go on?

In the Brown's home, the mother and father both workdays - mother as a waitress and Dad as a delivery truck driver. Their combined weekly income averages six hundred dollars. Both graduated from high school. The people in the Brown's home seldom talk with one another and never seem to have much of an idea about what any other family member is doing at the moment. The rules are very strict - I would go so far as to call them harsh. However, those rules are only enforced perhaps one time in fifty. Those are times when either Mr. or Mrs. Brown approach their wits end and then the punishment becomes overly severe and always involves the inflicting of extreme and prolonged physical pain. When questioned, the father is not sure which grade any of his children are in. The first time I visited in the Brown's home, the youngest child picked my pocket like a pro and the father thought it was hilarious. Well, again, I need not go further with this description, I suppose.

It is no surprise to you, of course, that the Smith's home was the well-structured, supportive and loving home of the fortunate youngster I have called John. Unlucky young Bob - fully equal to John, remember, in his inborn potential to become a happy, upstanding, productive and successful citizen - had been created out of the disorganized, mindless and hurtful environment of the Brown's home. John's parents had thoughtfully done a superior job of trouble-proofing their children. Bob's, of course, had done a superior job also - a superior job of mindlessly producing four, trouble-prone children, all doomed to sad lives of unending unhappiness both for themselves and for the rest of us whose lives and pocketbooks they will touch.

Did you see the word thoughtfully in my description of John's home and mindlessly in the description of Bob's? Children are never (well, almost never) trouble-proofed without parents or caretakers who go about the process of parenting in a thoughtful manner. By this I mean that they gather the most reliable information about child-rearing practices and mental health, and then carefully think it through together - as a team - and plan how to use that knowledge in ways that will be just right for each child in their care. They understand that being a parent involves considerable time each day spent in careful planning and in the evaluation of just how well things seem to be going. Being a good parent requires time - Planning time, Interaction time, and Evaluation time.

Children differ from one another in so many ways, and one of those has to do with which kinds of approaches from others they will accept and which ones they will reject or about which they will be skeptical. Having accurate and practical knowledge about children's' development, life, values and trouble proofing, is only one important step. Finding the appropriate approach to each individual child is equally as important because if the child won't buy what you're selling, the game is lost before it has begun.

This leads me to the fourth principle of how we become who we are. Most of us seem to have some inner spark, drive or purpose that moves us along through life. Some call it a spirit. To others it is motivation or will. To still others it is the basic essence or energy of each personality. The name is not important, here, but the concept is. We have all known, or at least heard about, people who possessed this tremendous spark. It allowed them to conquer overwhelming personal obstacles or to become all that they could possibly become as human beings against staggering odds - Helen Keller, Theodore Roosevelt, and Ray Charles, to name a few.

On the other hand, we have all known people who just gave up way before it seemed reasonable. Some have this tremendous will to succeed and to overcome the odds, while others don't. Those who do are indeed fortunate. Those who don't are often destined to live lives of mediocrity or even more likely, to experience far more unpleasant fates. The degree to which one possesses this spark, is an important, though elusive, ingredient in our formula for success as a human being. Some children seem almost able to trouble-proof themselves with very little outside help. Most cannot, however, so we must never just count on that happening naturally! We must never just trust to dumb (mindless) luck.

Along with a number of other procedures that we will soon examine, trouble proofing, then, relies on in-depth knowledge about these four principles of how we become who we are. It involves understanding the roles of: (1) inborn traits; (2) the influential experiences and circumstances in young children's lives; (3) the quality of those people and relationships that the children use as models; and (4) the nature and strength of that illusive inner spark that, when present, propels one toward unqualified success, or when absent, influences one to flounder as a failure. (If your child seems to lack this necessary inner spark, take heart. We will be finding some ways to help them learn how to guide and protect themselves anyway.)

Some basic philosophic tenets (values)

You now have the general flavor of what is involved in the trouble-proofing process. So, it is time to get down to the specifics. At the outset, it is essential to understand and accept the set of basic tenets or beliefs that underlie this program. I have previously referred to them as those that are at the core of the positive social philosophy, which I call, Reciprocal Esteem. You will need paper and pen or pencil from this point on. I suggest a spiral notebook, but any paper will work. You may recopy the information into such a permanent notebook later on. Please don't proceed beyond this point until you have note taking material in hand, otherwise the program's effectiveness will be weakened right from the start. (I will indicate what I think you should note. You may want to add other things.)

Since trouble proofing is based on a foundation of beliefs about human and social interaction, and since these beliefs must become second nature to the youngsters involved, it is essential that you, their most important and influential models, accept, master and practice these tenets first. Just how they are to be used will be presented a little later, although by the time we get there, I'm sure you will already have it pretty well figured out.

If you are a young person reading here in an attempt to trouble-proof yourself, I'm pleased to have you along and commend you for your effort. Just complete each step exactly as I suggest it. You may find it helpful to pretend that someday you may want or need to trouble-proof your own child or children and listen to this material as if you already were that parent. Later on, you will also want to read and re-read the chapter that was especially prepared for adolescents at the end of this program. (No fair peeking, now!)

From this point on I will, from time to time, present a positive statement and suggest that if you can agree with it, you write it down. Seldom have I found anyone who is truly interested in the welfare of our children who couldn't agree, but if, for some reason you find that you can't, remember that no one is forcing you to believe this way. Even so, you still may want to copy down the statement, but put it in parenthesis or print it instead of writing it or in some other way set it out as an idea to come back to and re-examine later.

The most basic tenet in Reciprocal Esteem, is this: I cannot ask anyone else to do helpful things for me, if I am not also willing to do helpful things for him or others.

It is actually a pledge not to be a selfish, greedy person who takes advantage of other human beings, isn't it? It says, that I will be reasonable in my relationships and requirements of others, that I will strive to strike a fair and just balance between what I ask for and what I am willing to offer. It says, "It's not fair to ask for more than I am also willing to give."

At given moments in our lives we often do need things or assistance from others that we cannot possibly also do for or give to others at that same moment. That must be understood to be both reasonable and expected. This tenet means that later on, when we do become able, we will be more than willing to do what we can for some other person who is in need. It doesn't even actually require that we pay back the specific person who has done something for us. It merely means that if I must request some thing or service now, I pledge to myself that I will be willing to perform for others, similar services that are within my ability later on when I am able to do so. Often, in fact, it may actually be a service that you have already performed for others.

Here are some examples. You find that you need someone to listen to you or to give you counsel on some matter of concern. When you seek out this help you must know inside yourself that you will also be willing to be the listener or counselor to others as such situations and requests may later arise and as your skill permits. Or, perhaps you find that you need some kind of information that you do not currently possess, so you go to someone whom you know can supply it. As you plan to do this you must know inside yourself that you are also willing to supply whatever kinds of information you may possess to those who may be in need of it. Or, it could be as simple as having an emergency arise, and you need a baby-sitter overnight. When you ask your trusted friend for his or her help in this matter, you must know, inside yourself, that you would also be willing to be inconvenienced in this or some similar way when a friend found him- or herself in a similar spot and needed to make such a request of you. We give and take in a fair manner.

People who grow up being willing to take advantage of others inflict the greatest kind of pains and agonies and extract the greatest, most devastating toll on society. We all have known takers and users who are more than willing to accept all the help and good things society has to offer, but seldom, if ever, even seem to consider that they have a responsibility, as a member of the human community, to in-turn act as a giver, doer and helper. They just drain us, don't they?

I suppose the opposite side of the coin that is implied here could be stated like this. I will only do, to other people, those kinds of things that I want done to myself. I will not steal from them if I do not want to be stolen from myself. I will not threaten, hurt, frighten or kill others if I do not want to be threatened, hurt, frightened or killed myself. Because the human Deep Mind finds it very difficult to deal with directives that are stated in the negative, we will not use this opposite, negative tenet. I think we do, however, need to understand its connection to the positive statement which, in a moment, I will ask you to write down and save and re-read often.

Although sharing our skills with others is a responsibility, I believe it is also a grand privilege to be able to help others in selfless (non-selfish) ways. In the first place, just to be this magnificent human being that we are is the most wonderful privilege in the entire universe. Nothing else, anywhere in the known universe, even comes close to the human being in its abilities to love, think, improve itself, and learn from its own mistakes and successes and the mistakes and successes of those who lived before, and to plan for the future, care for others, and build a better world and society for its own kind. Nothing else anywhere has this capacity to thoughtfully plan to improve the lot of the future generations of its own species. So, being helpful is a talent pretty much unique to the human species. Not to utilize it, then, does indeed, makes us less than fully human.

It is absolutely awesome to contemplate this Being that we are and the virtually boundless capacities that we possess in all of these areas. We are the only species anywhere in the known universe that has the capacity to actively promote peace among its own kind and to accept and enact a positive, helpful, caring philosophy of life. So, again, not to utilize these skills automatically makes us less than fully human.

To function at a level that is less than all of this, is to give up one's true humanity and to revert to the dog-eat-dog world of the lower animals in which survival goes only to the strong or deceitful. When we do function in terms of these unique and priceless human traits, survival can be made possible even for the weak and infirmed. When, as a group of caring human beings, we can help maintain the lives, comfort, happiness, success and ultimately, the self-fulfillment of those who are weaker than we are, we stand our tallest as human beings. We are exercising that remarkable skill of nurturing - of assisting even the weak to become all that they can possibly become. Strong or weak, humans not only have the in-born capacity to help one another, but we have the capacity to genuinely want to help one another. No other species, anywhere, can actually want to help others in this same way. What remarkable beings we are!

So, the basic tenet in our trouble-proofing program is to accept the concept that we must all help each other, and that to do otherwise, is the primary source of trouble-proneness. Without this helpful attitude, we have, instead, the inclination to take from others and use others unfairly in order to merely fulfill our own selfish ends. Without this basic belief in uniform sharing - sharing our skills, knowledge, compassion and protection for the betterment of all - the human race automatically divides itself into thieving, warring factions - each one trying to get the better of the others. We know it is true because we have all seen it happen in families, in neighborhoods, and between countries. If the study of history has one indisputable lesson for us, it seems to me that it is this: Distrustful, antagonistic, plundering, warring camps not only alienate and destroy each other, but in the end will surely destroy all of mankind itself. On the other hand, sharing, mutually supporting factions, enhance and improve each other, and build a bright, safe future for the present and the coming generations. No other approach can ever do this!

If this idea or tenet makes sense to you in a general way, then I ask you to write this down now: *I cannot ask anyone else to do helpful things for me, if I am not also willing to do helpful things for them or others.*

The second tenet or belief is this, and again, I will tell you when to copy it down: "I have a right to my life for as long as it naturally lasts." This is like saying, "Hey, out there. No one has a right to take my life or even to thoughtlessly endanger it." And, considering this belief in terms of the first and most basic tenet that we just discussed, it also means that I grant to all other human beings this same right to live their lives for as long as they naturally last, and that I must therefore act with due and thoughtful caution so as to not endanger their lives.

Sadly, many inner-city youths today will tell you they don't expect to live beyond age twenty. It has become a case of, "I have to kill them before they kill me and I'm smart enough to know I can't win every battle." It is as if they believe that they only have the right to their own life so long as they can protect themselves from their enemy's bullets, knife blades or brutal beatings. Youngsters have to somehow come to again believe that they and all humans have the right to live out their lives in safety. That is what this second tenet is about. It reminds us of how important it is to teach the youngest children and re-instill in the older ones this fundamental and essential belief in the absolute preciousness of all human life. Certainly, when a child doesn't think his own life is precious and has inherent value of and by itself, he will be unable to place much value on the lives of others. Not valuing life, he has no reason to refrain from destroying it - someone else's life or, most sadly of all, even his own.

So, learning to cherish his life and the lives others becomes the goal of the combined tenets one and two. How does a child learn to love himself and cherish his own life? By learning that the others who are important and influential in his life believe that he is a lovable and cherished being. Does he learn about his own preciousness by being put down, disparaged, punished, abused, injured, ignored, scorned, abandoned, belittled, yelled at, lied to, or allowed to fail as a human being? Does he learn about his own preciousness by being praised, loved, properly cared for, included, touched with tenderness, protected, respected, expected to excel to the limits of his ability, and to learn to abide by the rules that allow society to survive and flourish?

If this second tenet makes sense to you in a general way, and under most circumstances that you can foresee, then write this down now: *"I have a right to my life for as long as it naturally lasts, and I grant this same right to other human beings."*

The third tenet is this: Since, in order to have become the good person I am today I have needed the help of many other people along the way, I must now be willing to help others as they grow and mature and search after their way. None of us could have survived this long without the help of countless others. There are those who have produced our food; those who have protected our lives; those who have built our sidewalks, houses, schools and parks; those who have taught us important facts, concepts, and skills; those who have given us our home; helped conceive us, given birth to us, suckled us, bathed us, and clothed us as infants; those who have been eager and willing to be our friends; and on down a very long list.

Think about just how many of these helpful people you will never even meet or know by name. Think about the unknown people who brighten your days as they smile when you pass them on the street, or let you cross the intersection first, or apply their brakes just in time, or vote for socially positive legislation, or volunteer in ways that improve the quality of all human life in general, or work to discover lifesaving medicines, or protect your health by collecting and properly disposing of your trash, or inspect your food to keep it safe and healthful. Again, the list of these faceless helpers seems endless.

A few of these helper people, whom you have needed to use along your way, were paid for their services, of course, but many more were not. Both are important but it is the latter group - the voluntary helpers - on which I want us to model ourselves. Remember to smile at those you meet, to chat with the elderly lady sitting on her porch and the young paper carrier who comes to your door; to nod and mouth a message of thank you to the considerate motorist, to write a thank you note to those who attended to you when you required special help, to let a co-worker know how much you appreciate him, to find ways of telling your friends how much their attention and kindness mean to you, to let your family know that you appreciate those positive, helpful things they have done for you.

But more than any of this, the third tenet says that now it is your time - your turn, your opportunity - to freely give of your time, energy and assistance to those who are younger and frailer than you as they strive to find their way. We don't actually repay all those specific, helpful people from our own past, you see. We pass on that same kind of caring and helpfulness to the new generation. In this wonderful way, a steady supply of thoughtful helpers is assured for each new generation as it arrives on the human scene.

Some years ago I spent a short time working the counter at an ice-cream store. One day three teenage boys, out for a good summer day together, stopped by. During the process of getting their order they engaged in much horseplay and gave this old guy behind the counter a very hard time. Through it all I smiled to myself and handled each thing as it occurred with a calm and pleasant approach. After they left, a gentleman about my age approached the counter. He had watched the scene as it transpired and his assessment was to point out how disrespectful, rude, and inconsiderate the boys had been. He asked me how I could just be so kind to them. He would have refused them service and called security. My response was that I, too, had once upon a time been a mindless adolescent, for whom a good time at the moment easily overrode such things as respect and consideration. So, since many old men before me had taken the brunt of my own adolescent playfulness, it only seemed fair that it was now my turn to do the same. It wasn't that I approved of the boy's disrespectful behavior, but I did understand about teenage boys and that some amount of that kind of conduct is bound to take place even from basically nice kids. The observer had missed the boy's parting remarks: "You're OK, Pops, ya know. You're OK." I was pleased my time to be that patient old man had arrived and that I could remember how it had been. I still smile as I recall the incident and hear their fading laughter as they walked away, pushing and shoving one another, and just being the newest generation of teenage boys.

So, it is important to remember and be grateful for all of those people who have taken the time to be patient and helpful and thoughtful and instructive as we have grown up. To impart this concept to our children helps them begin to see how they fit into the flow of human history. Others unselfishly helped them along their pathway of life, and now it is their turn to unselfishly help others. Once they understand that like it or not, they are undeniably playing an essential role in man's social history, they must then begin evaluating the over-all productiveness or destructiveness of their own approach to life. This represents another major step in our progress toward producing a trouble-proofed child - a child learning to live up to his or her inner human potential, while resisting the temptation to merely function at the level of the lower animals.

Do children learn this concept and accept its humane implications by being taught they should ignore others, be distrustful of other's motives, or to live as self-sufficiently as possible? Do children learn this concept by remembering about those who helped them and taking steps to thank them when possible and thinking about that time when they, too, will be able to do those same kinds of helpful things for others? Constructive play gently guided along these lines will go a long way toward instilling this third tenet in very young children. Caring for baby dolls seems far more useful for this purpose than fantasizing with teen-age glamour dolls or aggressive action figures. Just plain old recurring conversations, in which you all remember the important people from the good old days, will be of subtle, though genuinely instructive benefit to the older children.

If this idea makes sense to you, then write this, now: *"Since, in order to have become the good person I am today I have needed the help of many other people along the way, I must now be willing to help others as they grow and mature and search after their way."*

The fourth tenet is this. Since, I need to be able to completely trust those around me, (and since I am not willing to ask others to be ways for me that I am not also willing to be for them), I must be completely trustworthy in all my interactions with others. Stop and think for a moment about how your World and life would change for the better if you never had to stop to wonder whether or not other people might be out to take advantage of you.

If you knew you could trust everyone you met life would be different in many wonderful ways, wouldn't it!

But that will never happen you may be thinking, and that may even be to some extent realistic. But, please don't allow your mind to take the next totally illogical step and convince you that since others aren't trustworthy you therefore have no responsibility to be trustworthy either. It can't possibly happen, if it doesn't begin somewhere, so why not with you and me! Even if we do still have to use good sense and judgment, about whom we trust, we can still always be trustworthy.

Trustworthy people gain positive reputations among most people. Deceitful people don't. Trustworthy people are sought after as friends and business associates and public officials and mates. From whom do you prefer to buy a car - someone you know you can trust or someone with a reputation for taking his customers for all he can? Who do you want as a significant other in your life - someone you can always count on to be trustworthy or someone you can't?

It is a strange thing about trust: So long as one continues to prove he is trustworthy we will continue to trust him, but if he shows himself to be untrustworthy only one time, we can never again truly be sure if we can trust him. This is one of the most frequent and important problem areas that occur between teens and their parents, and I mean that in both directions. The parent who sometimes can't be trusted is no less a problem for the adolescent than the teen, who sometimes can't be trusted, is for the parent.

Being a trustworthy person means that not only is your word always good, but that you can be trusted in a general sense to do the right things - obey the rules and laws and respect other people's property and rights and privileges. To be trustworthy means we can expect you to never take advantage of us in any way whatsoever. Picture a child who, by age twelve, has acquired this trait. Is he troubled-proofed? You bet he is, or at least he is well on his way. Who will you feel safest to have as your child's companion as they go off together to take in a movie - one who is trustworthy or one who is not? And if his companion is not trustworthy, how important is it that your child is? A trustworthy child has the best chance of resisting those so-called peer pressures that may try to influence him to go against the positive family (Human) values.

People pay special attention to the cheaters and tough guys of the world not because they are in any way respected in the true sense of the word, but because they are feared. People may follow them and cower in their presence out of dread and apprehension or because they may provide protection but not because they truly like the person or believe that he respects them or their rights in any way.

On the other hand, almost all of us pay attention to the trustworthy people of the world because we do, truly, respect them. Just as important as that, perhaps, is that we feel certain they respect us and respect our rights. We know they won't take advantage of us - even of our ignorance or weaknesses or other vulnerable areas. They make us comfortable. We like them. We certainly do not fear them. We seek them out as friends, because they have a positive and relaxing influence on us and on our lives. We feel safe in their presence. They help build a good world.

There are some folks, of course, who think one is somehow weak if he isn't out to take all he can possibly get at anyone else's expense and by virtually any means available. We see it in criminals, we see it in some businesspeople, we see it in some politicians, and we see it among some of our personal acquaintances. In some quarters the terms fear and respect, have merged into one terribly confused and socially dangerous concept. For these folks, winning means you always have to get the better of someone else. In essence they say: "For me to feel like I have won - that is to be respectable - I have to know that I have hurt someone else; that I humiliated him or I took his girlfriend or I put him out of business or I all but stole his property for the price I got him to take, and so on." They defend their own self-worth by thinking the terrible things they do are all okay since the other person should have been stronger or more attractive or should have known better. They make their own deceitful, non-trustable ways appear to be the fault, not of themselves, but of the poor dumb sucker they took advantage of or hurt.

This non-trusting way of life all seems pretty sick to me. I certainly cannot see how this reflects the truly wonderful human traits we can possess or how it moves us toward a comfortable, safe, happy, World. Instead, it again merely lowers us to the level of all the other animals. Why would we want to forgo our remarkable positive, nurturing human potential, and instead, struggle like wolves and vultures in the wilderness? It seems to me that to win as a human being means we do those things that make all of us winners - not just a select few. Mutual trust is a starting point. More than many may realize, it may well also be the finishing point.

We can't trust someone who we know is out to hurt us. Others can't trust us when they feel we are out to hurt them. When we set being trustworthy as one of our values, then we clearly pledge ourselves not to take advantage of others. Visualize a World in which no one attempted to take advantage of anyone else! A World in which all men, women and adolescents could be trusted. That World can never happen until we begin raising generation after generation of trustworthy human beings, can it?

To be trustworthy does not in any sense mean that we cannot be reasonably cautious ourselves about whom we trust. That is only smart in our world today - and that may be the saddest thing I have ever had to say about this World we live in - that we have to live our own lives as if others cannot be trusted. Sad indeed!

I, personally, decided long ago that I'd rather just go ahead and trust most people I met, knowing that I would be taken every once in a while by the bad guys, than to live my entire life in fear of the intentions of everyone I would meet. All in all, it has been a pretty fine trade-off, I think. "Within the limits of intelligent reason, I trust you, until you show me you are not trustworthy."

Some folks of course take the opposite approach. They choose not to trust anyone until they prove themselves to be trustworthy. It seems to me those folks protect themselves right out of so many wonderful relationships and fill their lives with day after day of worry and anxiety and suspicion and other negative feelings. They picture the World as a bad place and that must make for a very unpleasant, fear-filled, life. I choose to picture the World as a good place, and most every day of my life I have found it to be just that. Granted it is easier for me to do this in the heartland of America than it is in many other places in the World today.

Does this mean that I overlook war, poverty, crime, child abuse, hunger, drug addiction, mental illness, bullying, birth defects and the other terrible things that truly are out there in the World today? No, but it means that I do see the remarkable positive possibilities of people, acting in accordance with their grand potential as human beings, to meet and solve all of these problems, and that possibility makes the World Good. I trust, that somehow, we can find the way to help people tap their unique human gifts and work together for the betterment of all people everywhere. I believe that helping children grow into trustworthy beings is one grand step in the right direction.

Which of the following children will come to value being a trustworthy human being? Beth has parents who promise things they can never do or get or provide. They promise punishments or dire consequences that never occur. They brag about how they burned the guy in the car trade, how they use stamps from the office for personal use, how they fudged on their taxes, how they drove eighty five and never even saw a cop, how the dumb waitress forgot to charge them for the desserts so of course they didn't pay for them, and they belittled her brother for having returned a pair of shoes he found in a gym bag on a park bench.

Contrast that home with Karla's home. The parents are straightforward about what they can and cannot afford for the family. They tell the truth themselves and require it from their children. They always find ways so that at least one of them can attend each child's school activity or other special function. Family members ask permission before using something that is not theirs, and they are expected to carry out their responsibilities without being reminded. When answers to children's questions are not known, the parents admit it and find reliable sources that will provide them, rather than relying on speculation or mere opinion. All family members know they are expected to be honest.

I trust that you decided correctly about which family helped a child learn to value becoming a trustworthy human being. The models and expectations in Karla's home literally shouted out the message that trust was an absolute necessity for a successful life. Those in Beth's home declared just the opposite, didn't they? You may be interested to know that I became acquainted with Beth when she was seventeen and had been convicted of killing the clerk in a convenience store, which she and her boyfriend had robbed. Karla was eighteen when I met her and had just been the first minority teenager to be elected Governor of Girls State.

If, to value and promote trustworthiness makes sense to you, please write this now: *"Since I need to be able to completely trust those around me, I must be completely trustworthy in all my interactions with others."*

These next three tenets - numbers five, six, and seven - are closely related and overlap one another in several ways. They cover the areas I call approval, friendship and the mental health of one's friends and neighbors. Still, each one is distinct enough, I believe, to be stated and discussed individually.

Tenet five is this: "In order to survive emotionally and have a good life, I need approval from others, and I must therefore do my part by giving that same kind of approval to others."

There are really only three ways people can evaluate or regard each other: We can ignore others, we can approve of others, or we can disapprove of them. To be ignored is, for most human beings, the very worst type of social relationship because our very existence is not even being acknowledged. To be approved of is the very best type of social relationship because it not only acknowledges that we exist but that we exist as a deserving, worthy, compatible, acceptable human being. It means someone else thinks we are ok. To be disapproved of, falls somewhere in between being ignored and being approved of - usually closer to the being ignored end of the scale.

I have known many (MANY) trouble-prone children, who, when they felt they were being ignored by one or both of their parents, would intentionally misbehave. That is, they actively sought out the disapproval of their parents even knowing it might result in harsh physical punishment because at least then their existence was being acknowledged - they were being noticed. If they couldn't figure out how to win positive approval, which they certainly preferred, they would settle for recognition through disapproval rather than being completely disregarded.

I have also known many youngsters who have similar feelings about society in general. Rather than let society just go on its way without ever seeming to care or even recognize that he exists, many a teenager, for example has done outrageous things. They may be as harmless as outlandish hair do's and strange clothing, or as serious as out and out violent criminal acts, including arson, homicide and suicide.

Trouble-proofed kids know, without any doubt, that they have the approval of those who should be important to them. Trouble-prone kids most often do not. Not having the approval of those significant others, can lead to at least two devastating outcomes. First, the child comes to believe that he must not have the kind of good points that can be approved of by those closest to him - parents, siblings, teachers, and so on. This is usually enough to prove to a child that he is no good, so he just stops trying to be one of the good guys, and by default, trouble begins to enter his life on a daily basis.

The Second, frequent outcome of not feeling the approval from parent figures and others from whom it should be expected, is that he is then forced to seek that approval elsewhere. If he has given up expecting to receive approval for his good points, he does whatever it takes to gain approval from some other group that he comes to define as now being important to him. This is usually a group of similarly disapproved of age-mates - the ultimate in poor role models and unsuitable sources for approval.

What would be a normal, fairly typical way to feel about a family or a society that rejected you? Many would, quite naturally become angry, even revenge minded, or in the least, be unconcerned about the welfare of those who had rejected them. When one feels society in general has rejected him, then anyone and everyone can become his target or at least be seen as not deserving of his concern. These feelings make it easy to begin stealing, harassing, and even hurting those people. It allows a sense of detachment so one doesn't have to feel sorry or guilty about the hurtful things one does to them.

Often, all of this also serves another purpose: By arousing the active disapproval of society or parents, it moves one up the ladder from merely being ignored to suddenly gaining the higher status of being openly disapproved of. Admittedly, still a very sad state of affairs, but a not at all unfamiliar situation. Being somebody thereby often comes to mean being somebody others fear, hate or are at least annoyed at.

So, it seems obvious that we all need to feel the approval of those who we should be able to love and who we hope love us. Since, according to Tenet One, we don't ask for such things without being willing to participate on the giving end as well, we must do what? We must freely give our approval to those around us, especially to the children who are still searching to find out what kind of person we think they are or can become.

One major caution is in order when it comes to handing out approval. Only give your approval to things you truly feel are positive, good, right and correct. Never appear to be approving of things you truly can't support. We can love the trouble-prone child and we can let him know we love him regardless of how he acts, but that love for him and our disapproval of those troublesome behaviors must be seen by us and by him as two very different things. Said another way, just because we love him doesn't also mean that we automatically approve of his socially destructive behaviors. Said still another way, we can love him but not like his behaviors, or as more frequently stated, we can love him although we don't like him.

It is extremely important to find things, however small, that we can openly and frequently approve of in all those with whom we have dealings - just be sure they are honest and realistic. When we must verbally disapprove of or disagree with something done by someone else (which is certainly both reasonable and necessary, sometimes), it is always best to begin our response by pointing out something about that person of which you can approve. This gives the other person a degree of tolerance, if not respect, for you and what you will soon be pointing out to him. It begins the interchange on a positive note. It draws him into the message.

For example, if you disapprove of your child swearing in your home, rather than just calling him down for the bad language or immediately instituting some punishment, you might try saying something like this. "You know, Austin, you have such a wonderful way with words, and such a fine vocabulary, I would hope you could find more meaningful and challenging and acceptable ways to express yourself than through swearing. In fact, I expect you to begin using that great head of yours to do just that so long as you are within ear shot of me, or else I'll have to take some steps that I guarantee will help you remember not to swear around here. Do you understand what I am saying to you?" (By the way, why didn't I prohibit swearing everywhere and not just within my earshot? Because such a rule would be totally unenforceable and unenforceable rules are always harmful to the child's wellbeing. See my book, *The One Rule Plan for Family Happiness*, for a more complete discussion of this and other more useful kinds of rules.)

Another approach that implies approval of the child, spouse, or anyone else for that matter, is just to always ask for and listen to their side of the issue first. You may actually learn something that will help you see the problem in a new light. In the least, the other person will feel that you respect his right to have his say or offer his explanation. Then, if you must still disagree or disapprove, you might begin in this way. "I must say that I'm impressed with how well you have been able to state your point of view, and I'm glad I listened to it. Now, I'm sure that you will show me that same degree of respect by also listening to what I have to say. ..."

Avoid, at all cost, using that disastrous confrontation causing word, "but," in such discussions. You know how it goes, "What you say may be true, **but** here's the way it really is." Such confrontations can be easily changed into useful discussions by merely changing that confrontation word, "but," to the cooperation word," and". "What you say may be true, and I think an open-minded person like you will also find this other point of view interesting." In the first case, the word, *but*, sent the universal signal, "this has now become an argument and I must use this time while he is talking to figure out my next point or defense." In the second case, the word, *and*, sent the universal signal, "this is a rational discussion from which we both may learn something if we just listen and try to understand one another." *But*, almost always signals total disapproval, and builds a wall - an argumentative base. *And*, always signals some degree of approval and acceptance, and builds a cooperative base - a bridge that beckons the other to keep listening.

Fifteen years ago, Tommy's Dad had high hopes that his athletically skilled ten-year-old would grow into a talented baseball player. So, the father took it upon himself to point out all of Tommy's errors to the boy, intending, in that way, to improve his various skills. To his Father's amazement, Tommy soon lost interest in baseball and only continued at his Father's forceful insistence. No activity is much fun if you don't receive feedback that you are doing well or, in the least, improving a little - that is, get back some kind of approval for your efforts. With no approval, Tommy gave up.

Twenty years ago, James appeared to have average athletic talent but loved to play baseball. With encouragement from his parents, and a coach who always let him know what he had done right or just a bit better than before, James eventually became the first string third baseman on his high school's team. His ball playing brought great joy to him and his entire family. With approval, James blossomed and his relationships within the family and with his school mates brought him feelings of respect, and happiness, and self-worth.

The first boy, Tommy, was killed in an attempted filling station hold-up when he was fifteen. James is now a proud and competent husband and father and is himself a much beloved, always encouraging, little league coach. Did these boys' eventual success or failure hinge just on this one point? Of course not, but the stories illustrate the more basic approach of the two living environments and that was the pivotal point.

Without obvious and frequent, realistic approval from

others, young people have essentially no chance of approving of themselves. Without self-approval, there cannot be a mentally healthy person. Without good mental health, there cannot be happiness or self-fulfillment. Without the approval of those people who are important to the child and, therefore, not having gained the capacity to approve of himself, there can be no trouble-proofed youngster.

So, if you can agree about the importance of this fifth tenet, please write this, now: *"In order to survive emotionally and have a good life, I need approval from others, and I must therefore do my part by giving that same kind of approval to others."*

The sixth tenet can be stated this way: "Since I need good friends in order to survive and to enjoy life as a well-adjusted person, I also must be, and, in fact, want to be a good friend to the others in my life."

One of the unique qualities possessed by the human being is the capacity for friendship. The degree to which we are able to do this, sets us apart from, and above, *almost* all other animal species. We have this ability and need to search out several other people with whom we can feel extremely close. As a species, we humans find it essential to share with, confide in, aid, support, and love other special people. In my little book entitled, Loves Several Faces, I have developed this topic further, so I won't re-cover that same ground here except to suggest how it applies to trouble-proofing kids. [Now included in the book Life as a Precious Gift]

When we know, without any doubt, that someone other than a relative truly cares about us, our feelings of self-worth grow by leaps and bounds. Relatives, we often think, are obligated to like us, and if they didn't, they might even feel guilty. So, although it is great to know parents and siblings and uncles and aunts love us, it is particularly reaffirming to know that others who in no way have to, also love us. We call these people our special or close friends, don't we?

Think about it for a moment - the person with at least one or two really close personal relationships of the kind in which friendship flows freely back and forth in both directions is usually a pretty happy, well-adjusted person. To qualify as a close or special friend in the most accurate sense of the term, an individual must possess four characteristics. First, he must be willing to accept (that is, to approve of) the other person all quite unconditionally. This means that a friend cares about you as a precious human being regardless of your little flaws or little mood swings or other idiosyncrasies. With a friend, you don't have to be perfect and he will love you anyway. In fact, with a friend, one of the really nice things is that you don't have to constantly be on guard to hide those little imperfections because you know he isn't going to use them to judge your worth as a person. He isn't going to make your perfection a condition of the relationship.

Second, a friend wants to do things for his friends - big things as well as all of those little things that will help make the other's life easier, brighter or more meaningful. He is always there when you need help and you can always feel comfortable about asking for his help because you both know that you would do the same for him in a second.

Third, a friend must be able to allow his friends to give to him in the same ways he gives to his friends. People need to give of themselves to others. It makes us feel worthwhile and unselfish. A true friend allows us to practice this trait on him, so that we may feel the satisfaction that giving brings to us. This represents another uniquely human trait - that of being able to be charitable - and when we don't find ways to demonstrate our charitable side, we feel uneasily less than human way down inside our Deep Mind. It is a kind of uneasiness that instills a sense of general anxiety just under the surface, the source of which many folks never discover, so they just have to live forever with that uncomfortable, gnawing, unsettled feeling. They know something is missing in their life, but they just can't figure out what it is. When I sense this is one of the problems for someone who has come to me for help, I suggest that he or she begin some regular and frequent volunteer activity. It is amazing how, within a matter of weeks, that terrible sense of uneasiness and emptiness just vanishes!

Fourth, a friend is honest with us and we can count on him to answer us truthfully and to put us in our place when that is needed. A true friendship survives, and in fact thrives on, constructive criticism. From a true friend we can accept those unflattering truths about ourselves that we might have great difficulty accepting from anyone else. Why? Because we know that friend always has our best interests at heart. We believe that whatever he has to say to us is done with the most loving intentions. A friend is truthful with us and we accept those truths gratefully.

Friendship, then, is a basic human need. It must be a two-way relationship, in which both parties show genuine affection for one another, are eager to both give and take the good things that can come of such a relationship, are able to be truthful with one another, and find it easy to see through each other's imperfections to the goodness that lies 'inside'.

Children who learn, early in life, that friendship involves all of these things, soon come to treasure such open, honest, comfortable, non-self-centered relationships, and acquire the priceless foundations of altruism. Altruism simply means the ability to put some other person's needs first - when that is necessary or appropriate - or even just for the pure pleasure of seeing someone else happy or safe or comfortable or in some other kind of improved condition. We human beings are the only life form in all of the known universe that can do this, and, since we do possess that ability we are not living up to our positive human potential until we are regularly practicing this remarkable and most rewarding skill - altruism.

There is a distinct and important difference between merely being a friendly person - that is a pleasant, easy to get along with person - and having the capacity to be a true friend in all four of the senses just described. Perhaps sociable would be preferred to friendly as we typically use that word. Sociable people may be quite pleasant and easy to relate with on the surface, but that doesn't automatically qualify them as having the four essential traits necessary to be a true and special friend. In fact, many sociable people turn out to be people-users, rather than friends. Youngsters often confuse the two and may, from time to time, need adult help to discover the difference before they get deeply hurt.

Children who have the capacity to be true friends almost universally come from homes in which the parents provide the friendship model. As they see their parents enjoying the friendship relationship in all four of its dimensions, they are soon caught up in the spirit themselves. The model is always the best teacher, though some aspects of friendship are so subtle that they may need to be specifically pointed out or taught to youngsters. On the other hand, sometimes we adults can learn much about the unconditional aspect of friendship from watching our children.

A youngster who possesses the desire and genuine ability to be a true friend is again well on his way to becoming a Trouble-Proofed Kid. True, many solid friendships similar to the type just described do exist among gang members and between others who associate for the purpose of doing harm to outsiders. The point here is that without this ability to feel absolutely loyal and altruistic toward some other revered person, positive human relationships are not possible. It is the purpose of the other tenets to provide the necessary positive social motivation that leads the youngster away from the destructive, trouble-prone, social motivation seen in such negative gang relationships.

So, if you can agree that friendship, in all of these senses of the word, is an important tenet, please write this now. *"Since I need good friends in order to survive and to enjoy life as a well-adjusted person, I also must be, and, in fact, want to be, a good friend to the others in my life."*

The seventh tenet could well be split in two, but the ideas are so closely tied together that I am going to present them as one concept. It goes like this: "Keeping those people around me well-adjusted will increase my chances for a happy life, and since positive strokes and tenderness are needed for good adjustment, every day I will give large doses of those things to those around me."

You see how this one first makes a statement about the importance of mental health, and then also provides a method for helping achieve it. Let's speak first about the advantages of living among well-adjusted people.

Roscoe and Frank are ten-year-olds who are both

experiencing great difficulty adjusting to a new school. Roscoe lives in a home where errors and mistakes are expected as a normal part of growing up and where useful problem-solving techniques are known by all and always utilized when difficulties occur. When a problem arises, his father is often heard to say, "Well, what do you need to learn so that this situation doesn't have to occur again?" Roscoe seldom has to be punished because he is eager to improve himself and learn how to avoid previous errors. The family laughs together a lot and each day is filled with hugs and kisses, snuggling and smiles. The family members are honest, though tactful, about each other's flaws, and are always enthusiastic in their praise of each other's accomplishments and good points. Roscoe's family members genuinely like one another.

In his home, Frank is frequently spanked for his errors and is currently enduring a two-month grounding for fighting at school. When his father is not around, however, his mother doesn't enforce the grounding. It is a home filled with yelling, blaming and hurting one another. Frank's questions are seldom answered. His parents point out to family and friends alike that Frank has become a very unpleasant child to have around and that they fully expect him to end up in jail someday. His father drinks himself to sleep every night and his mother spends the evening sitting quietly in front of the TV, chain smoking and withdrawing more and more from the life she finds so distressing. Frank cannot remember ever being kissed or hugged by his father.

Tell me now, which child has the better chance of eventually adjusting to life in the new school? Which one may well find this to be a turning point in his life, leading to perpetual social maladjustment? And why do we all immediately and so easily know the correct answers to those two questions? We know because we understand that it is very difficult for Frank to live and improve himself when surrounded by his maladjusted family members. We know that it is so much easier for Roscoe to learn how to handle his problems with the kinds of support available from the mentally healthy people with whom he lives.

For all the compassion we may feel toward them, the fact remains that poorly adjusted people are usually burdensome, insensitive, unpleasant, even irritating Beings to have around. They tend to magnify the little, normal troubles you already have and in general, contribute to the disordering of your life. And all of this does not even address the more serious issue of how they tend to hurt or destroy those who are closest to them and those who must depend upon them, like their children.

Poorly adjusted people also become a tremendous financial drain on society. We have to pay to protect ourselves from their attacks or thievery, pay for the destruction of property and loss of life they cause when inebriated or otherwise out of control, financially support them and their children when they are unable to keep a job, and in all the many other support and mental health services you can imagine.

The point is, a poorly adjusted person is not just a problem for that person himself or even just for his immediate family, but eventually his sickness may affect many more of us. Whether we are the kind of person who truly desires to help those folks so they can become happier people, or we are the kind who merely wants to be rid of the financial drain and personal burden they put upon us all, we can readily agree that it makes good sense to help others improve their overall social and personal adjustment.

It makes perfect sense to most of us that maladjusted children are going to be trouble-prone and that well-adjusted children are far more likely to be trouble-proofed. Since trouble-prone children tend to have unfavorable effects even on good kids, their mere existence out there in our child's world makes our child's life less safe and more difficult. Since maladjusted children most often (though not always) come from homes with maladjusted parents, it makes sense to help those parents improve their own adjustment or in the least learn how to improve their child rearing techniques.

It cannot be the function of this book to present a full-blown mental health course or to provide a complete child-rearing program. I do urge the interested participant to seek out such information if they feel the need for it. My book, *The One Rule Plan for Family Happiness*, may be of some assistance. Most of my books have as their basic purpose the improvement of life and human relationships.

It *is* the purpose here, however, to emphasize, that when your responses to life and its problems don't seem to be working for you - that is, don't seem to be solving things and improving life and replacing sadness with happiness or failure with success - that you should seek help from a mental health professional. A trusted clergyman may be a good starting point or the counselor or social worker or psychologist at your school or at your child's school. Just don't put it off. There are ways to get back on the track to happiness and a good life.

It is not difficult for reasonable people to agree that good adjustment is a state we should all seek and that maladjustment, wherever it occurs, is a sad and socially devastating condition about which we all must be actively concerned. But, what can one person do to solve the rampant mental health problems of the World? Let's begin with the little things and leave the big things to the professionals. And don't fool yourself; it is often those so-called little things that turn out to be far and away the most important!

The second half of our tenet states: "since positive strokes and tenderness are needed for good adjustment, every day I will give large doses of those things to those around me." It is my studied and sincere belief, that if, each day, we would each increase by just ten, the number of positive strokes we give to those outside of our home, we would have an unbelievably positive impact on the mental health of all men, women and children everywhere. I would bet (if I were a betting man) that we would quickly reduce the patient load of mental health professionals by seventy-five percent!

How could this be? It is simply because a huge percent of poorly adjusted people just don't feel important, or worthwhile, or significant to others. They don't feel included in the *family of man*. Also, because as we each begin planning about and dispensing positive strokes, we suddenly and permanently grow to view ourselves as nice guys and therefore value our own self-worth more than ever before.

That actual percentage of improvement can be argued up

or down forever, of course, but that isn't even the point is it? The point is that - without any doubt - we each improve our feelings of self-esteem and therefore our overall adjustment, when others respond to us in positive, approving ways, and when we know we have contributed in some positive way to the lives of others. There is no more certain way to improve another's good feelings about himself and about others than by being one of those others who freely and sincerely hand out positive strokes to those encountered on one's daily rounds.

What constitutes a positive stroke? Any *deserved* compliment is a powerful positive stroke, and it is this that we usually think about when we hear the term. But there are other acts that also fit this category. A simple smile is a grand positive stroke for some. A helpful deed such as holding a parcel as someone fumbles for their keys is another. Providing directions when asked or when you see someone is obviously in a quandary. An arm for the elderly or physically challenged as they cross the street or mount the curb. A bright, "Hello," a meaningful "Thank you," a pleasant and cheery, "Beautiful day, isn't it," are all ways to tell others that you acknowledge their presence as an important person in your life at that moment and that you truly do want things to be going well for them.

So, a positive stroke is anything we say or do that builds someone else up and makes him realize that we appreciate or value him, or that he possesses a skill or ability or feature that we recognize is praiseworthy or valuable. A positive stroke is a kind of approval, isn't it? I previously spoke about the importance of realistic approval, and much of that discussion can be transferred here, so I won't persist.

Tenderness is a positive, usually welcomed, method of approaching another person. It can be in the tone of one's voice or in the choice of words one uses. It can be demonstrated in actual physical contact - in the gentle handshake or the kindly hand on the shoulder or the tender, yet firm and genuine, embrace. For most of us a tender approach is interpreted as a comfortable, non-threatening gesture, suggesting kindness and good intentions, as contrasted with a harsh or aggressive or over-powering approach which may be distasteful or irritating or indicate threatening or questionable intentions.

For some, of course, tenderness is seen as a sign of weakness, and they rush to try and take advantage of that person. A tender person need not be weak; in fact, some of the most powerful, forceful, influential people I have ever known have been among the most tender I have ever met - Joe Louis, Mohammed Ali, Eleanor Roosevelt, Sam Walton, Linus Pauling, Jimmy Carter. So, don't fall for the illogical argument that a tender person is therefore also a weak person.

Children who live with tenderness and with ample positive strokes have a fine opportunity to become trouble proofed kids. For sure and certain those who live with harshness and degrading, or humiliating strokes have the very best chance of becoming trouble-prone kids.

So, if these dual ideas of assisting others to improve their level of personal and social adjustment, and that one simple and effective way of moving folks in that direction is through the dispensing of positive strokes in tender ways, then please write this, now: *"Keeping those around me well-adjusted will increase my chances for a happy life, and since positive strokes and tenderness are needed for good adjustment, every day, I will give large doses of those things to the people around me."*

Tenet eight is this: "I have the right and obligation to become a competent, self-fulfilled human being (a builder), and I must grant others this same right and encourage them in their attempts."

By "competent" I mean things such as proficient, skilled, effective, capable, accomplished, and well learned. By self-fulfilled, I mean that we feel good about ourselves, because we have found some things we are good at and enjoy doing, and that we have worked hard to become all that we can become in those areas. It may seem obvious that we have this right to become competent and self-fulfilled, but why would I say that we have this obligation or duty, as well? Let's back up a step or so.

In other books, I have described several categories into which most people can be placed regarding the effect they have on society. One is the *User*. The User takes advantage of others, using them in whatever ways fit his selfish purposes and without regard for the welfare of that other person. The *Observer* is a person who just sits on the sidelines of life, watching it pass by but without ever jumping in and getting involved or making a difference. Although he may never actually do specific harm to anyone, he most certainly makes no useful contribution to society. In some ways his inaction may well be harmful as he fails to support educational or charitable or political or research efforts that could benefit the rest of us (as well as himself). A third approach is that of the *Destroyer*, who takes what he wants regardless of who or what gets hurt, damaged, or eliminated in the process. As is obvious, none of these three categories is helpful to the survival or improvement of society, and, in fact, each in its own ways damages and consumes society.

The fourth category is the *Builder* - the one who uses his uniquely human talents and insights to renew, improve, and enrich society and the human species. It is my point of view, that because as human beings we have the innate positive capacity to be Builders, it is therefore our responsibility and obligation to do so. Only the Builder can protect and improve the human species and it seems important to me that we do just that. It seems to me that each person should take advantage of his or her own special talents in order to become all that he can become as a human being. To do less lets himself down as well as the rest of us. It leaves him at the unfinished level of just another being (animal).

This is, of course, my value and belief and may not be yours. But, even if you prefer to just sit around in your underwear and watch TV and really can't agree that we should each strive to be all that we can be, could you agree at least, that we should not intentionally get in the way of other human beings who are trying to find ways of becoming all that they can become? I have found that most reasonable and thoughtful people agree with this.

So, even if you do not feel that you have an obligation to become all that this human being, which you are, can possibly become, you probably do agree that it would be wrong to interfere with another human being's right to try to become all that he or she can possibly become. This assumes, of course, that this other person continues on the path of being or becoming a Builder.

All trouble-prone kids fall into one of the negative categories. They are either a User, an Observer, or a Destroyer. None ever come from the Builder category. By contrast, all trouble-proofed kids are members of the Builder category, as are well over 95 percent of their parents. (What about that nice kid next door, who, one day blows away his neighbor? I guarantee a search of his true situation will demonstrate he was not a truly committed builder.)

There is just no way to emphasize strongly enough the importance of valuing and modeling the approach and beliefs of the Builders. Builders do positive things that make life and living pleasanter, easier, safer, more fulfilling, more comfortable and more predictable for themselves and for all of us. Builders think about the future of the planet, the human species, and the social order. They realize how precious and very special this human species is and strive to protect it, to nurture it, to improve it, and to help it reach the very pinnacle of its potential. To do less is to reject, or at least to ignore, the very meaning of being a human.

Again, let's examine two real children from two actual homes. Sara's family encourages and enjoys reading and searching for answers to the questions that come up in their frequent discussions about every imaginable topic. They contribute as a family to several charities and all do volunteer work at various community agencies. Sara's mother is on the school board and her father - a cook in a local restaurant - coaches youth soccer. Sara plays violin in the youth symphony. Her older brother plays football and has just held a one-man show of his oil paintings at the local gallery. Her younger sister is in Girl Scouts and busies herself inventing labor saving devises for the housekeepers of the world. They are each a unique individual, and one might wonder how they all could possibly come from the same family. They laugh together often, as well as have heated discussions about topics of mutual concern. Each one has developed along those lines made possible by his or her special talents and interests. Sara also paints and plays softball, and although she does both poorly, she enjoys them a great deal just because she thinks they are fun. I could go on, but this is enough to provide the essential flavor for this family.

Colleen's family is also real. They are quite well-to-do, financially, having four cars and two boats, a magnificent big house and pool, beautiful, fashionable clothes and electronic games and gadgets coming out their ears. They seldom talk among themselves and could not tell you much about what any other family member valued or believed or what their personal goals might be. Movies, TV, electronic games and boating are their main leisure time activities. Colleen enjoys cruising Main Street on Saturday night in her late model convertible, yelling obscenities at the less fortunate and making fun of the elderly out for their evening walks. They belong to the Country Club but have very few close friends. They show up at church as a family every Sunday morning. Colleen and her two sisters have no idea what they might want to study in college, though they assume that's what they will probably do after graduating from high school. During the special telecasting of a recent momentously important historic moment, her father called the TV station to complain because they were pre-empting his favorite sitcom rerun. I could go on, but it hurts too much!

Which parents have had to repeatedly bail their children out of jail? Which family was recently named Family of the Year by the local Chamber of Commerce for having made their community a better place in which to live? Since we're on a roll of correct answers here, let me try just one more. Was it necessary to have lots of money and lots of stuff in order to build character and be positive role models and to live together as a wonderfully happy, helpful, family?

I suppose I should add here, that I have known many wealthy families that also produced caring, law abiding, Builder-type children. Money, one way or the other, is not the point. Those parents would have produced trouble-proofed kids even if they had been penniless, living in tarpaper shacks. Once the basic necessities of life can be consistently provided, additional money is irrelevant to the success of this trouble-proofing activity. Three of the nicest, most self-fulfilled, well-balanced, socially helpful youngsters I have ever known, were the children of a poverty-stricken mother from a terribly impoverished inner-city area. But that mother knew what living the good life was really all about, and she modeled it in her own values and behavior, and she demanded it from her children every single day. I respect her - Katy Somers - as much as any person I have ever known. She lives the Reciprocal Esteem philosophy to its fullest, and in the process, she changed her entire neighborhood for the better.

A World filled with Builders will be a simply glorious place - Beautiful, safe, cooperative, comfortable, satisfying, self-fulfilling, and populated only by trouble-proofed kids and their proud, effective, loving families - all the things it can never be when populated by Users, Observers and Destroyers.

If you can agree with this general tenet, please write it down now. *"I have the right and obligation to become a competent, self-fulfilled human being (a builder), and I must grant others this same right and encourage them in their attempts."*

Tenet Summary

Those are the eight most basic tenets, which I believe comprise the minimal set needed for the parent who is serious about raising trouble-proofed kids. This implies that not only are these the tenets the child must come to learn and accept in order to be safe but that first, the parents must accept them, must practice them, must always model them, and must frequently talk with the child about them in open, honest, and practical ways.

Taken together they represent the social philosophy I call Reciprocal Esteem, which can now be more simply stated this way. *We all respect one another's basic human rights, and always only do to, and for, each other those things that we thoughtfully believe will be best for all concerned, in the long run.* These eight tenets help define the two words, "rights" and "best."

Let us now review them one more time here, and I suggest that the serious student of this approach review them each and every day - preferably each morning in order to get his mind set in the right direction. And once the child becomes involved in learning these tenets it is important that the parent and child review them together each day and talk about how they think they are doing in regard to achieving each one. Where there are problems, help the child work toward realistic solutions that are appropriate for his or her age and abilities. Set daily goals for yourself and have the child do the same. Get quite specific about how you are each going to achieve each of the tenets most every day.

So, now, let's look at them again.

The First tenet states.   I cannot ask anyone else to do helpful things for me if I am not also willing to do helpful things for him or others.   This is a prime characteristic of the Builder Personality and is the exact opposite from the prime characteristic of the User, the Observer and the Destroyer, all three of whom always put their own selfish interests ahead of everyone else's.

Second, the Builder believes, I have the right to my life for as long as it naturally lasts and (under most circumstances) I must grant all others this same right. The User will protect someone's life so long as that person is useful to him, but then, once used, will show neither caring nor mercy. The Destroyer sees what he wants and takes it with no regard whatsoever for the life or wellbeing of anyone standing in the way. The Observer would certainly watch someone else being harmed, and might or might not actually enjoy it, but would never come to his or her aid.

A Third belief of the Builders of the World is this. Since, in order to have become the good person who I am today, I have needed the help of many other people along the way, I must be willing to help others as they grow and mature and search after their way. The Users would certainly agree that they need the help of others and they constantly take advantage of others in this regard, but to then feel any obligation to be helpful in return would make no sense to them. The Destroyers would typically feel they are self-made men so owe no one anything. The Observer is never tuned into giving, of course, and is usually so distant and unlikable that no more than the necessary number of other people have probably ever helped him directly in the first place.

Fourth: Since I need to be able to completely trust those around me, (and since I am not willing to ask others to be ways for me that I am not also willing to be for them), I must be completely trustworthy in all my interactions with others. The whole concept of trust is virtually irrelevant to the Observer, since he avoids meaningful interaction of all kinds. The User works hard to gain your trust so he can then take advantage of you and laugh in your face about your having been so gullible as to fall for his line. The Destroyer usually makes no pretense of being trustworthy himself and almost never trusts anyone else, which is what he must do to survive, since so many folks would like to see him severely punished, if not maimed or put out of the way permanently.

Fifth, the Builder fully understands that in order to survive emotionally and have a good life I need approval from others, and I must therefore do my part by giving that same kind of approval to others. Neither Users nor Destroyers approve of anyone else, and it is certainly doubtful that deep down inside they even ever truly approve of themselves. Observers are often so depressed that approval seems just too effort-filled and probably meaningless. None of these three negative personalities can ever know and understand the wonder-filled feeling of having won someone else's approval through those unique and priceless human traits of unselfish kindness, love, and personal accomplishment.

Sixth: Since I need good friends in order to survive and to enjoy life as a well-adjusted person, I also must be, and, in fact, want to be a good friend to the others in my life. Again, due to the aloofness of the Observer, friendship is just immaterial. He neither gives nor takes in order to maintain a friendship. The User feeds on taking advantage of friendships, so, although he may appear to be quite expert at forming close personal relationships, they are always insincere and designed for his greedy benefit only. The Destroyer may engage in friendship-like relationships - strategic alliances would better describe them - in order to get what he wants when he doesn't believe he has enough power himself to just crush someone. Destroyers never know the joys, responsibilities, and privileges of true friendship.

Seventh: Keeping those around me well-adjusted will increase my chances for a happy life, and since positive strokes and tenderness are needed for good adjustment, every day I will give large doses of those things to those around me. The Observers make no attempts to influence others in any meaningful way, so the underlying concept of this seventh tenet is meaningless to them. Users are often willing to join any cause that will promote their own personal comfort, so they will usually buy into the idea that making others better adjusted can make their own life easier. They just don't want the rest of us to become so well adjusted that we tend to see through their own selfish motivation. Destroyers don't buy the "helping" idea at all. When they find someone who irritates them, they just destroy them. Why mess around with rehabilitation when, "poof," and they're out of the way forever? After all, the Destroyer never values the lives of those who stand in his way.

And finally, here is the Eighth tenet. I have the right and obligation to become a competent, self-fulfilled human being (a Builder), and I must grant others this same right, and encourage them in their attempts. Users and Destroyers see those of us who pursue personal excellence as total wimps, who fail to understand that the acquisition of bunches and bunches of stuff and the wielding of absolute power is all that really counts in this life. The observer, not ever getting involved in life, may know he has the right to improve himself, but he certainly feels no obligation to ever do so. He seems content to remain a bump on the log of life.

I am certain that by now you understand where I think humanity and this precious World of ours will end up, if, generation after generation we continue to produce Users, Destroyers and Observers instead of Builders. The only for sure and certain trouble-proofed child, is the one being raised by a Builder and who is, himself, learning to accept the Builder's philosophy and the Builder's approach to life and living it.

Chapter Two

It is no big secret that the child's World today is filled with conflicting values that are in obvious, direct, and constant competition with these eight, trouble-proofing tenets. TV, music, video games, the business and sports ethics which teach that to win at all costs is all that is important, and deteriorating elements of the youth culture, itself, all scream opposing values at our children.

Flip through the TV channels any evening, during two, of the prime-time hours, or stroll through any video game arcade for five minutes, and we witness how the value of life is presented as a cheapened and devalued commodity - how easily and thoughtlessly and violently it is snuffed out with apparently not so much as a second thought. The soaps teach us that trust is a fantasy that just doesn't exist, and that all that is really important is the physical, sensual side of life, and taking whatever you want. Much of the music is filled with violence and phrases that reduce the wonders of love and sexual intimacy to that of fleeting, vulgar, dirty acts of power or a prestige-gaining sport, rather than of lasting, mutual tenderness, respect, and caring.

Listen in on the conversations of even the so-called good

kids between the ages of ten and twenty and hear them scheming to cheat and lie and deceive. It seems to be undertaken with no twinges of guilt or concern about right and wrong - just about the chances they may or may not get caught. Listen to them extol the accepted virtues of taking massive revenge on another for the wrongdoing done to them. Listen to the foul, vulgar, demeaning language they use as they describe their enemies, young and old, and especially those of the opposite sex who have slighted them in some way. Listen as they, also, reduce sexual intimacy to a power-based, prestige-gaining, dirty-minded sport. Listen to them plan senseless, drunken weekends of escape, rather than self-fulfilling, growth producing activities.

Now, I may sound like some overly self-righteous, circuit riding, Bible thumping preacher, out of the Old West. I truly don't intend to sound that way. I do intend to point out as dramatically and realistically as possible, that as parents we must understand that there are these powerful conflicting realities out there in our children's World with which our cherished values must somehow be able to compete.

How the human mind operates.

In order to mount a plan of action that has any chance of success we must be knowledgeable about how children learn values and how those values come to guide their thinking and planning and, eventually, their conduct, itself. To this end, let me take a few pages here to summarize the way our minds operate and to suggest some nearly fool-proof, trouble-proofing methods that follow directly from these principles. For those of you who are familiar with some of my other books this may provide a review of information you have already mastered. For those who are not, you may later want to clarify some of these points by working though The Secrets of Deep Mind Mastery, The One Rule Plan for Family Happiness and How to achieve Deep Down Forever Happiness.

The deep part of a person's mind is ultimately always in control of all he or she does. If you often find yourself doing things which, a few minutes later you know were wrong or dumb or at least inappropriate, it probably keeps occurring because you don't understand two very important things about yourself. First, how your Deep Mind operates; and Second, how to help your Deep Mind direct you along the path you want or need to be headed. These same things apply to your children, of course, and these principles will assist you to help them learn how to appropriately come to guide themselves.

Everyone needs to fully understand three of the several major characteristics of their Deep Mind. (I'm speaking here about people from about age nine or ten and older.) These all relate to how you tell your Deep Mind what kind of a person you want it to help you be. In order for it to carry out your wishes it needs to receive very clear and consistent instructions from you. I call these instructions, *directives*. A bit later, I'll have more to say about just exactly how one goes about talking with his or her Deep Mind.

The first of these three important characteristics, I call THE RECENCY LAW. This means that under most circumstances, the most recent directive that you have given your Deep Mind is the one it will most likely believe is true and will therefore use in guiding your conduct. Here is an example most of us have experienced. Suppose it is one of your goals to always tell the truth, and usually you do just that. But, recall a time when you stretched the truth a bit. And then, in order to protect that little fib you had to tell another one. Remember how much easier it was to tell the second one than to tell the first one. And the third - well, that one was probably a breeze. Very likely it just rolled off your tongue as if you had been used to lying all your life. Why this change in the ease of telling lies? Simple! That first fib alerted your Deep Mind to the possibility that you may be giving it some new general directive. So, when the second lie was contemplated, the Deep Mind went along a bit easier. (If you will recall, it had fought you on the first one. You may have felt guilty or hot, or your breathing may have become more rapid or your mouth may have become dry.) But the second was a bit easier, and by the time you were thinking about the third lie your Deep Mind was already hard at work helping you prepare the tale so it would be as believable as possible. You see, the Deep Mind works according to the most recent message - directive - it thinks (assumes) you have sent it. This is why it is SO important to know what kind of person you want to be and never deviate from that plan. Let that first twinge of guilt or anxiety that your Deep Mind sends you remind you to get yourself back on track before you ruin things and send your Deep Mind into major reorganization.

The second characteristic is what I call THE INTENSITY LAW. Although the Deep Mind usually listens most clearly to your most recent directive, as just suggested, it also tends to listen even harder to the directives that are set into it with the most force, the most intensity, accompanied by the most emotion. This is why fears are often so much more powerful, as directors of our behavior, than is our logic and reason and common sense. We know that a cockroach, a spider, or a mouse is probably not going to do us any harm, and yet, because our reactions to them have often been sent to our Deep Mind accompanied by fear (when we were very young, perhaps), we still react to that fear directive. This tends to occur even though we may have more recently tried to tell our Deep Mind to, "grow up and act its age about this cockroach thing." Directives set into the Deep Mind with intense emotion will usually overpower the Recency Law. (There are techniques that can banish those irrational reactions quickly. Again, I direct you to my book entitled, The Secrets of Deep Mind Mastery).

The third characteristic I call THE POSITIVE-DATA-ONLY LAW. The Deep Mind is set up to respond to positive phrases only. (Just why this occurs is also explained in the book mentioned above.) It hates to receive negative directives because, again, unless they are accompanied by intense emotion - so intense as to be downright hurtful - the Deep Mind either ignores the message altogether or takes it upon itself to re-interpret it as a positive statement. Words such as "Don't" and "Never," become "Do" and "Always." Example: "Do not under any circumstances within the next five seconds think about dripping, oozing, spurting red blood!" And, so, tell me, what are you thinking about right now? Of course, about dripping, oozing, spurting red blood! The Deep Mind worked its magic and made DO NOT become DO. Don't play with the new kids next door! (Thirty minutes later where may your child be?) Never play with matches! Don't smoke, don't drink, don't take drugs. Just say no! All very well-intentioned instructions but they all represent total ignorance of how the human Deep Mind operates.

When negatives are necessary as temporary safety measures, the person who has learned to trust you because you have proved you are always trustworthy, will go along with your negative request for a short time until you can provide the necessary information and examples that will prove your point. Non-trustworthy people have, of course, lost all these battles way before they begin. And, since normal teenagers will insist that black is white just for the delightful sport of it, negatives absolutely always and forevermore backfire as attempts to control or even mildly influence the adolescent. So, when approaching your Deep Mind, or that of someone else, steer away from the negative and toward the positive.

Fortunately for all of us the Deep Mind is born with one pre-programmed prime directive at its core. Above all else the Deep Mind has as its major task that of protecting us and keeping us from physical harm. When we have found ourselves in danger, we have all experienced how the focus of our attention narrows and all we can think about is safety or survival. That is our Deep Mind taking over and acting according to its most important Prime Directive.

There are, however, a whole variety of problems that we must regularly face other than life and death situations. Since it is virtually impossible to have pre-programmed your Deep Mind to be ready for every individual and unique situation or problem that may present itself in life, how can you prepare it to do the right thing for you as new threats or circumstances arise? The answer is actually quite simple. Make sure that you provide it with one or two, broad, PRIME DIRECTIVES of your own. These are those elements of your value system or philosophy of life that are the most important guidelines you have for yourself, for your life, for the way you always want to interact with your fellow human beings. Most likely, these will also be those elements of your value system that you want to pass on to your children.

As an example of what I mean here, my own personal prime directive is: "To love comes above all else." My Deep Mind is well aware of this all-important aspect of my approach to life, so in many situations it can just rely on this Prime Directive to help it make its decisions. I suppose a secondary prime directive, of mine, would be: "Always be accepting of and inquisitive about that which is new or different or unclear." This leads me to try to better understand things fully before I make judgments about them. Since my built-in Physical Survival prime directive will easily over-ride these when I am in physical danger, I am automatically protected from making personally dangerous use of either one of them.

I am not suggesting that these Prime Directives of mine should be your prime directives, but I use them to illustrate how the Deep Mind can operate more smoothly and logically and consistently for you once it fully understands what you believe is most important. If you don't yet know what you believe, I urge you to get to work on it and find out.

The daily mental tune up

Now that you understand how important it is to talk with your Deep Mind in positive ways, and that emotionally powerful and recent messages help it understand your wishes the easiest, you need to set up a regular routine to keep it up to date on your wishes. I call this process the daily mental tune-up. First thing every morning, I get very comfortable, close my eyes, and review with my Deep Mind my several prime directives and my basic values and beliefs about how I think I should relate to other people as I go about the new day. Sometimes I ask my Deep Mind to work on some particular problem or topic, such as, "Today, let's take advantage of every opportunity that arises to help Jay come to realize what a lovable person he is." My tune-up usually takes only two or three minutes and seldom more than five. Making it a daily ritual takes advantage of the Recency Law. Visualizing each value or behavior with intense feelings of love, compassion, nurture, or whatever, utilizes the Intensity Law. And stating things in the positive, keeps my Deep Mind from becoming confused and having to reformulate my intentions in distorted ways. (The Deep Mind prefers images and emotions to words.)

And this Daily Tune-up time is THE best way to combat all of those negative, anti-value processes, which are continually going on in the World of your Child. For one to know what he believes is right and wrong is fine – essential, even.   But without regular reminders sent to his Deep Mind, all of the child's many daily experiences to the contrary, tell the Deep Mind - through the action of the Recency Law - that that prime directive or value is being changed.

Think about how many times each day a child's World exposes him or her to acts of violence and wrong-doing that are presented as approved or normal or at least commonly expected behaviors - television, newspaper, music, playground, actual events in the streets of your town or city. It has been estimated that a typical ten-year-old, from an average, middle-class neighborhood, witnesses between twelve and forty such apparently approved violent encounters each day. Somehow, his daily tune-up has to be powerful enough to overpower this barrage of constant and more recent encounters. This is why it is absolutely essential that we make value conversations a customary part of our daily routine with our children. In the morning we help them plan ways to live up to their values and in the evening, we encourage them to recount the ways in which they actually carried them out. As the child leaves the house, rather than telling him to behave himself it may be more useful to ask him something such as, "What kind of guy are you going to be today, sweetie?" When he responds, he is reinforcing his own prime directive.

Other ways to reinforce values

While talking, discussing, planning and recounting are all useful, worthwhile, and important aspects of trouble-proofing your child, by and away the most important aspect is modeling. The child who starts and ends his day, every day, in the presence of an adult who consistently models these values - the eight tenets - has the very best chance of becoming trouble-proofed. All the talking, preaching and Bible or Koran thumping in the World will never be as powerful and influential as what the child actually sees taking place.

Does preaching about good health habits and weight control to his son, carry anywhere near the same amount of influence coming from an overweight father as it would coming from one who is slim and trim? Of course, not. Does the unreliable and, therefore, untrustworthy parent, stand much of a chance as she preaches to her daughter about the virtues of always acting in honest ways? Of course, not. When a child recognizes that the parents' actions suggest that they don't truly believe in the values they are verbally promoting, then any child with an ounce of intelligence will certainly not be convinced that they are actually important. There is an age-old adage that seems pretty accurate: "Children believe what they see, not what they hear." Assuming you are an outstanding model, you already have a large part of this trouble-proofing struggle won.

If, as a parent, you can only enact one aspect of this entire trouble-proofing program, I believe that it must be this: *Always be an open and genuine model of these eight, trouble-proofing tenets.* If you can't do this, then be certain your child has another adult in his or her life who can consistently, on a daily basis, do so in such a powerful and believable way as to overshadow your own weakness. It can't ever be as complete or as convincing as if you were the model, but it will be far better than nothing, at all.

The 'myth' of peer pressure

Now let me turn to the topic of peer pressure. Parents shudder and teens get sick to their stomachs at the mere mention of this frightening subject. I'm here to tell you that Peer Pressure is a myth, well, almost a myth, anyway! Let's begin with a story.

Jerry and Kyle are thirteen. Neither one has been in much trouble yet, although they live next door to each other in a neighborhood in which most teenagers eventually end up as certified juvenile delinquents. They share many of the same friends, and like most boys this age, they enjoy spending large amounts of time with them - often outside of their homes.

Jerry also regularly spends time with his parents - they have breakfast and dinner together at the kitchen table every single day. They usually enjoy these times together and continue to be able to talk about almost any topic - they recall past good times together and listen to each other's dreams and plans for the future. Jerry tells his parents about his friends and how it is to be thirteen these days. His parents recall how that may be the same or different from when they were his age. They talk about honesty, right and wrong, trust, and how privileges are always dependent upon how well a person (of any age) handles his or her responsibilities. On more than one occasion Jerry has asked them questions about drugs and about sex and other kinds of boy-girl relationships. His parents have always been pleased to answer them.

At thirteen, there is no doubt in Jerry's mind as to what his parents believe about how a person should live his life. He is beginning to form a very solid picture of who he is, what kind of person he wants to become, and what he believes about life and living it appropriately. He feels good all over when he knows he has lived up to his own true beliefs about such things (integrity), and feels terrible and empty inside when he realizes he has let himself slip and disobey one of the rules (values) he has set for himself.

Kyle can't remember the last time he sat down to a meal with his family - they either eat on the run, or in the living room while watching TV. When he talks to his parents it's usually to con them out of money and when they speak to him it is usually in anger and loud enough for the neighbors to hear. Kyle does sleep at home - at least most nights - but that's about all the time he would choose to spend there. He can't tell you for sure what his father does at work. Kyle has no idea what a value is, let alone what his or his parent's values might be. When he has questions about getting along in the World or about the growing up changes taking place within him, he goes to his street friends for advice and information (or misinformation, as it all too frequently turns out!).

On one Saturday night not long ago both Jerry and Kyle were on the street corner talking with their friends and messing around, commenting on the "features" of all the girls who passed as guys that age have always done and probably always will. Bruce, the oldest and most influential one in the group, suggested that they break into old Mr. Stein's bakery and trash the place. (Mr. Stein had repeatedly asked them to leave his store, since they seldom purchased anything, and their language and horseplay made it quite unpleasant for his older, regular, paying customers.)

Without hesitating, Kyle went along with the idea, agreeing that it would be fun, even though inside he knew it was over-reacting to Mr. Stein's actions and understood that he could get into big trouble if caught. Also, without hesitating, Jerry said, "No thanks, guys. You're all going to be in big trouble and what you're thinking of doing just isn't right." He left the group immediately, went home and played cards with his family. Kyle and the others were soon on probation. Bruce was confined to the Juvenile Detention Hall for six months. Mr. Stein went bankrupt when he could not afford to remodel the bakery after the boys vandalized it. Jerry is living happily ever after.

Both Kyle and Jerry knew that vandalism was wrong. Still, Kyle went along with the group. Later, to the juvenile judge, Kyle blamed his actions on irresistible peer pressure. Why was it peer pressure to Kyle and just a dumb idea to Jerry? Why did Kyle feel he had to go along in order to remain one of the group and Jerry didn't even give that side of it a second thought? Why was friendship more important for Kyle than right and wrong?

Probably because it was more important for Jerry to remain his own friend - to be true to his own important self-guidance beliefs. For Kyle (who had developed no important, self-guidance beliefs) to be liked by his friends at any cost was all he had to direct his behavior. Jerry's feelings of self-worth were based on living up to what good things he expected from himself. Kyle's feelings of self-worth were totally dependent upon what his friends thought about him.

So, rather than dismissing such misbehaviors as merely being caused by peer pressure, and thereby concluding that it is not really the misbehaver's problem, perhaps we need to begin describing such events as a specific deficiency of those all-important self-guidance values in the misbehaver himself. Instead of concocting alibis for the wrong-doer by invoking that mystical influence called peer pressure, we can far more profitably focus on the actual missing traits within the wrong-doer. We must find ways of instilling those absolutely necessary values and beliefs, that are variously referred to as; "inner strength," or "strength of character," or "a value based life-style," or "positive self-guidance," or "belief in what seems right for all concerned," or in plain old-fashioned terms, "just wanting to be good because it's the right thing to do."

Positive values become a child's portable control system. Rules from home that are immediately unenforceable once the child leaves home, provide no real guidance at all.

The myth, then, is this. Rather than being a case of peer pressure it seems to me that it is a case of value deficiency. True, at certain ages, the influence of one's age-mates is profound, but time and time again I meet youngsters whose value strength is so powerful that the whole idea of peer pressure is truly nothing but myth. If these strong, self-knowledgeable kids can, at any given moment, put the following of their own rules about right and wrong ahead of some need for peer acceptance so can yours once they have had the opportunity to learn the technique. I believe that Trouble-Proofing provides that formula.

The S.A.F.E. Technique

In the chapter for young people, which accompanies this program, I teach them what I call the S.A.F.E TECHNIQUE. By using each of the four letters in the word SAFE as a memory guide, a four-step method is outlined for youngsters to refer to when faced with situations which may have the potential to produce trouble. At this point I want to present a summary of that technique, but I refer you to that specific chapter so you will understand exactly what is being suggested to the young people.

'S' stands for STOP and SCORE the SITUATION. Stop and Score the Situation for its trouble producing potential. If you have any doubt that it is not clearly safe or right, then immediately score it as possible trouble and stay away from it. If, even for a moment, you hear that little voice inside saying that it may not be right or safe, then don't get involved any further. Think about the very worst thing that could happen in that situation and then decide if that would mean trouble for you. If it would, get out of that situation as quickly as possible. You have no way of knowing ahead of time that that worst thing won't actually happen. Don't get sucked into to playing the odds by telling yourself that there is only one chance in ten that something could go wrong. That one chance in ten or even in fifty is more than enough to stop yourself right there. Say that you do give into those one in ten odds on ten different occasions during a month's time. Since one in ten means just that, you can count on getting into big trouble at least one of those ten times and maybe even more often than that. If there is any chance it's wrong or could harm you or someone else, do something else. Make this one of your personal conduct rules and you will be well on your way to staying out of trouble.

'A' stands for ANALYZE. Analyze what, if any, of your needs at that moment would be met if you went ahead and did this activity, or went into this place, or whatever. Often it might seem to satisfy such needs as excitement, or entertainment, or flirting with danger, or a chance to prove you are brave or courageous or skillful at something - maybe impressing someone of the opposite sex. Whether we like to believe it or not, those are all normal needs in young people. So, here in step two, just make a quick list of which of your needs might be satisfied by this particular activity or circumstance.

'F' stands for FIND. Find other ways for meeting those very same needs in safer ways that you believe are also right rather than wrong. If it is excitement you are after at the moment and that need tempts you to go ahead and do this thing you really know you should not do, then find an acceptable, alternate way to have some excitement right then or in the very near future. If the need is to be accepted by your friends, then think about what kind of friends you really want to have - those who demand that you go against your values or those who allow you to live up to your values. Then, go find some friends who will not require you to tempt trouble or personal harm. It is always a good idea to have a list or a menu of activities that will meet each one of your major needs. They must be well in line with what you believe about right and wrong and must take your safety and the safety of others into consideration. Then, when you feel the need for entertainment or feeling powerful or proving that you are charming, or whatever it may be, go to that menu to find an acceptable activity that will do just that! Responsible parents help youngsters understand this and even assist them in making such a menu.

'E' stands for ESTEEM. In this case, Esteem simply means being able to be proud of yourself for obeying the rules of life that you have set for yourself. Self-esteem is the feeling one gets inside when he knows he has lived up to his own highest expectations for himself. Self-disgust or self-hatred is the opposite. After you have scored the situation for possible trouble, analyzed why it seems attractive to you - that is, what needs it may be tempting - and after you have found another way to satisfy that same need so you have been able to walk away from the potentially trouble producing situation, then you can Esteem yourself. Feel yourself just filled with self-ESTEEM both because you were wise enough to keep out of trouble and because you were smart enough to find other ways to meet those normal needs and urges you had been feeling.

Self-esteem, self-confidence and self-appraisal

Back in the early days of my professional career when I was interning in what was then called an "orphanage" for the homeless children of veterans, I experienced this dilemma. I administered a self-esteem inventory - it's like a test - to two eleven-year-old boys - Jim and Bill. They both received scores that showed they each had exceptionally high, positive self-esteem. This meant that each one liked himself a lot, just the way he was. My dilemma was this. Jim was a well-adjusted leader of his age group who was admired and respected by most all of the other eleven-year-olds. Bill, on the other hand, was the biggest troublemaker in the home, constantly in hot water for stealing, fighting and vandalism. How could both of these youngsters possibly score high on a measure of self-esteem? I was baffled. I thought self-esteem indicated good mental health and adequate personal adjustment.

The concept of self-esteem is, in many ways, a strange one. The guys who want to be good guys feel self-esteem for being good guys, and the guys who want to be bad guys feel self-esteem, or something closely resembling it, for being bad guys. Whenever one lives up to his own concept of the kind person he wants to be, he tends to feel good about himself. So adequate, socially beneficial adjustment requires more than just any old variety of self-esteem. It requires the kind of self-esteem, which flows naturally from the eight basic tenets or values we talked about earlier.

Jim and Bill both liked themselves as they were, so both had high self-esteem. A third boy, Jake, who was also constantly in trouble, scored extremely low on the self-esteem scale. Who do you suppose would be more open to learning a new set of more socially acceptable behaviors - Bad boy Bill or bad boy Jake? Since Jake's low self-esteem suggested he didn't like the way he was behaving, he would most likely be the one to make good progress in a behavior change program. The truth is, he did, and by his freshman year, Jake was elected class vice-president. By that time, Bill had been shipped off to what back then was called a reform school. Did Jake's low self-esteem scores improve as his behavior changed? They sure did! Can a youngster who is raised among law-breaking or violent models have high self-esteem? Certainly, if he accepts and incorporates those anti-social behaviors into his value system. So, high self-esteem is not - as many would have us believe - the whole picture in this trouble-proofing process.

During childhood, and especially adolescence, self-esteem is a very fragile and fleeting feeling. A youngster, finding some success or sensing admiration from some important person will be brimming over with it one minute, only to drop to the depths of despair ten minutes later when there still is no call, as promised, from the boyfriend or girlfriend.

Self-confidence is a somewhat separate concept from self-esteem, although the two are often linked. The self-confident teenage male may, for example, become so cocky that he feels invincible - as if nothing at all could ever happen to him - and so, feeling that way, he takes dangerous, mindless risks. That kind of reckless self-confidence is not what we, as parents or childcare takers, are hoping for. This dangerous, unrealistic, variety, easily promotes the belief that good luck is with him, and believe me, any unrealistically self-confident teenager who at the same time believes good luck is with him, is in immediate danger. In that state he will try things that at any other time, even he would recognize as stupid - but not at that moment, not in that lucky, invincible frame of mind.

Through the years it has become all too obvious to me that juvenile detention home residents universally trust in luck, while well adjusted, hardworking, trouble-proofed teens, almost never trust to luck.

It becomes essential, then to help teenagers learn to differentiate between those times when they are foolishly counting on luck (questionable odds) and those times when they are wisely counting on their own hard work, solid facts or at least on common sense that is not inconsistent with solid facts. A good question to ask a teen when he seems to be unrealistically overconfident or is counting on luck goes something like this, modified to fit the specific youngster's situation, of course: "If your little brother were to try that same thing, would you just let him?" You see, most teens can see the dangers involved when loved ones absurdly count on luck or act too cocky, just not when they, themselves, do.

Asking this question in a straightforward, unemotional way, often makes the youngster stop to reconsider his own actions. It certainly works better than calling him stupid or crazy, which, with an adolescent just forces him to continue what he's doing whether he really wants to or not. Face saving is *all-important* at that age - often more important, even, than their fear of harming themselves. And even if they answer that question with, "No. Why would I care what happened to that little jerk?" you better believe that, regardless, inside that teenage head the right wheels *have* been set in motion. In this case, never argue with a "No." Just back off and carefully observe from afar. Of course, if the youngster is obviously in danger you would immediately take appropriate steps to ensure his safety.

So, appropriate self-esteem and self-confidence are both necessarily based on the eight tenets and must be guided by realistic self-appraisal. Realistic self-appraisal comes about through years of protected and successful trial and error learning. By protected, I mean situations in which the child will not harm himself or others as he makes his attempts. Trial and error learning simply refers to those times when one keeps trying new solutions, one after another, until he finally comes up with one that works. Several failures or perhaps even hundreds of failures may be needed before one's approach becomes refined and corrected enough to perfect the proper answer or solution. It is the way most of us learn most things.

The always present personal mistakes and social blunders of adolescence will be far less traumatic when children have learned this simple lesson, early in life. Trial and error learning is useful and the errors one makes along life's way are not bad things but are actually useful signposts about what to avoid the next time. The process of realistic self-appraisal often cannot develop for children who have grown up being put down or consistently blamed for every little honest error. For them, trial and error has not been allowed, so when it has not been trial and success, it has, instead, been trial and punishment or at least, trial and put down. This produces human beings that are reluctant to try new, unproven paths, and processes. They have little confidence in their own abilities to find good solutions so they have to go along with those ideas that others - most often their peers - may suggest. They don't even think in terms of looking for several possible alternative solutions because that is not how they have been taught to think.

'There are always *two* sides to every issue' - a very dangerous concept

How often have we heard it? How often have we even said it? "There are always two sides to every issue!" This is an example of how the language you use - of how the language your elders taught you to use, really - can get you into the biggest of problems. It provides a well-practiced, though dangerous, deep mind directive.

When Jake was eleven, he was faced with a dilemma that most youngsters never have to face (thank goodness!). The choice he was given was this: Jake could either graduate from high school at the end of the year and (as a money-poor boy) take a scholarship being offered to him at the state university two hundred miles away, *or* continue to stay in high school until he got older. (You see, the brain with which he was born just happened to learn a lot faster than the brains of most kids, so Jake had completed all the required schoolwork well ahead of time.)

Not liking either of these alternatives (the so called, two sides to this issue), Jake looked further, and found that there were several more sides available to consider. He could try to gain a scholarship at the local college so he could stay at home where an eleven-year-old boy belonged. He could get a half time scholarship so he could go to college half days and remain in high school with kids he knew the other half-day. Better yet, perhaps, he could go to college half days and return way back to sixth grade where his real, same age, friends were, for the other half-day. He might go to the local college, either part or full time and work for spending money at the grocery store where he already worked part time. Let's see. There were at least how many "sides" to that issue? I count about seven, and there turned out to be even more.

Jake found an alternative that worked very well considering the totally unnatural situation with which he had to deal. My point is this. If Jake had stopped after finding just TWO sides to the issue (the way the school officials had done) he would never have found the most satisfactory arrangement. (That turned out to be attending the local college full time, working at the grocery early mornings for spending money, returning to his neighborhood to play with his friends after school and weekends, and continuing to live with his family.)

So, I encourage you to carefully teach your children to never be automatically content with just two sides to an issue. Continue searching until you have uncovered the third and tenth and perhaps seventy-fifth. Who knows how many sides there may be. Much of the advertising world succeeds because they know we tend to be content with just two sides - theirs (the right one, of course) and brand X (the wrong one, naturally). Politicians play this game all the time in their campaigns. They ask, "Do you want my opponent's poor plan, or my great plan?" Perhaps we need to tell them, "I'd rather have one of these other plans that neither of you has yet suggested."

Hate mongers count on this characteristic also. They would have us think that, "You either like them (the other group) or you hate them - it's just that simple." Perhaps another useful alternative would be to find a way to get to know them better, study about their history, their problems, and their goals. Perhaps go and live among them so you can truly understand them. Then you may be in a position to make a decision about liking or hating. Probably you would find you like some of them and don't like others of them - that would be a whole lot like the people who make up your own group, wouldn't it.

Out in the child's world there will be many occasions when someone or some group will make it appear that EITHER he must be for something OR against it. The trouble-proofed child understands that anytime he hears that limiting "either/or" red flag, he must immediately begin to look further and find additional possibilities. The myth contained in the statement, "Either you break into the store with us or you will look like some kind of wimp," is immediately dispelled and made powerless, when the child adds some appropriate additional alternatives himself. "I'll end up in jail. I'll be breaking the law. I'll be hurting someone who has never done me any harm. I'll be doing something that is contrary to everything I believe is right and good. I'll be allowing my friends to get into terrible trouble. I'll be disappointing my family." He always searches for additional sides to the issue. It makes a great (and often humorous, when taken to extremes) game at the dinner table and provides excellent trouble-proofing practice.

Well, the lesson is to train our children to just keep on looking and never be tricked into thinking that two sides ever, under any normal circumstances, give you the total picture or all of the reasonable, necessary, and legitimate choices. Not even in the heads or tails situation is there always only a set of just two choices - I once witnessed the flip of a quarter and it ended up standing on end after a short roll.

Opinion vs. Fact

The first time I got sent into the hall by a teacher occurred early during the first day of first grade (and I had not attended kindergarten!). She had asked me, "How do you think a light bulb works?" I responded: "It really doesn't matter what I think because that could be wrong. But I do know a book where we could look it up so we could all be sure." Well, back in 1943 that was disrespect of the highest caliber, so into the hall I went! Perhaps she was trying to stimulate our creative thinking (though I didn't believe that then and don't to this day!). What she was doing, however, was lulling her students into believing that opinions were at least as important as facts when it came to problem solving or understanding the World.

I continue to be at least amused, if not often seriously bothered, by the conversations I over-hear in the workplace, at restaurants, and in social gatherings. It seems everyone has opinions, but very few seek out the actual facts - or even consider that doing so would be the sensible approach! Many don't even seem to understand that there probably exists a set of reliable facts somewhere, which they could consult in order to find an accurate answer. How can this be? They all went to school. What went wrong along the way? To me it is a scary state of affairs that so many folks, especially young people, live their lives apparently unknowingly substituting opinion for available facts!

Not long ago I overheard a discussion about obesity. There was a nurse in the group who presented a brief, thirty-second, well founded presentation of the scientifically established genetic and social factors involved. Those "facts" were met with these "opinions" from the three others involved in the discussion. "I don't buy that. I think it's just eating too much." "Everybody knows when you overeat you gain weight." "Wire their damn jaws shut, that'll thin 'em down in a hurry." The actual, scientifically discovered facts held absolutely no influence, no power, and no authority. They were not interested in hearing the established facts. They placed more credibility in their own opinion than in science.

I don't mean to imply that opinions are never appropriate. Personal judgments of like and dislike and suitability are often both fun and proper. My point is that we must know when we need hard facts and when mere opinions will do. We must learn to ask ourselves this question. "Is this a topic where opinions will be safe for me and others (such as about art, music, literature, friendship, sports loyalty, and similar topics.), or are facts necessary to provide a true, just, or validly established answer (in areas such as health and diet, science, government, child-rearing, and mental health)?"

This seems to be part of a more universal trend, these days, not to respect experts of any kind. It appears to me, that to a large degree, the experts have brought this on themselves - or perhaps I should say ourselves. During the past fifty years or so the information-gulf between the super-educated and the minimally educated has grown fantastically wide. There is an obvious social gulf that has accompanied this as well. In general, the super-educated live far away from the real-life events and circumstances of the less well educated. The super-educated, therefore, tend to be unable to provide realistic, life-practical suggestions and easily understandable information to the masses. Their unsuitable quality of counsel is virtually useless, and so, it is all just ignored or even made fun of - and often rightly so.

It seems such a frightening situation that the less-expert people of the world - a far, far larger group than the experts - have just written off this essential aspect of human progress and survival we call accurately established knowledge. Somehow, we must rekindle a respect for knowledge across all educational and socioeconomic levels. If we don't, humanity, like the man in the blinding snowstorm who died three feet from his front door, will surely perish. [Some of the above was taken from my book, *A Crisis of Myths*.]

Naturally, trouble-proofed kids, those who just turn out that way because the parents seem to have a natural feel for it all, typically come from homes in which knowledge is treasured and respected. Early in life the children in these homes learn the difference between opinion and fact and in which circumstances each is and is not appropriate. These children will never rely on the folklore of their peer culture - myths and unfounded coincidences that have been turned into fact by the uninformed. Children who are precise thinkers and easily separate fact from opinion or fiction have a far better chance at becoming and remaining trouble proofed.

It is fun and growth producing to play mental games about why we think things happen or how certain things might have come about, but it is important not to stop there with opinion. Always take that essential next step and check it out. Discover the facts and see how close to being accurate you were. It is a great way to expand your mind, your knowledge, and help your children remain trouble-free.

Fifteen-year-old Jack tells his new girlfriend, Betty, that if she sits in a tub of hot water after they have sex, she can't get pregnant and therefore, it won't be necessary for him to wear a condom. How does he know this is true? His friend, Sam told him. Did he make any attempt to verify it with an authority like a physician, or look up contraceptive methods at the library or on the internet? No. He just went with the folklore of his age group. Would a trouble-proofed kid stop there? You can bet that he would not. Jack's girlfriend got pregnant. Jack left town. Reliance on verifiable knowledge can and does prevent such heartache. Acting on unfounded opinion or rumor almost always causes heartache. Learning to tell the difference, trouble-proofs.

Summary

Before leaving this section let me just recap several things we want to be sure to include in our trouble-proofing program. With all of the negative values floating around in the child's world today, bombarding him in an almost moment by moment fashion, it is absolutely essential that we help our children learn and accept the eight tenets, that they develop and practice one or two strong prime directives, and that they set aside time each day for their mental tune-up (and understand why that is absolutely necessary). Remember, that there is no more influential teacher of values, than the parent who strives to consistently act as a perfect model for the children. I spoke about peer pressure as a myth. I replaced it with the concept of value deficiency, which is the condition that exists when a child does not believe strongly enough in the principles of right and good and therefore finds himself unable to direct himself along the appropriate paths when associating with trouble-bound friends.

I outlined the S A F E technique and its four steps to be used by youngsters in new or possibly troublesome situations. The child learns to stop and score the situation for its trouble potential. He analyzes it by asking himself which of his needs that situation looks like it might meet. He finds safe and sensible alternative ways to meet those same needs, and then esteems himself for having lived up to his values and having stayed out of trouble.

I spoke about the dangers of fecklessly overly self-confident youngsters, especially teens, who so frequently couple that feeling of invincibility with trusting to luck, and how realistic self-appraisal is to be encouraged by viewing one's own actions as if they were those of a loved one. I suggested how important it is to form the habit of looking beyond only one or even two sides of an issue, and how necessary it is for children to learn how to separate opinion and folklore from well-established fact. I urged you to find ways to help your children trust and revere accurate knowledge and to help them learn how to find it and to want to use it regularly. If in doubt as to how to go about this, just ask your local librarian. She or he will be pleased to help and will only respect you for asking. Always have time to answer your child's questions and if you don't know an answer or aren't sure you have given the full answer, just admit that and set a time to look it all up. Make it legitimate to admit one doesn't know everything and make it important to then take that essential next step and find the proper, accurate answer (the way they come to see you doing.). Do these things and your children will be among the most fortunate in the World.

Throughout the remainder of this book, we will illustrate exactly how to make this approach work for you. I will present a multitude of real-life examples and answer the most frequently asked questions.

Chapter Three

During the workshops that I present on this trouble-proofing topic for parents, educators, child welfare workers, law enforcement officers and other groups of interested people, it is at about this point that I hear the following questions:

"Ok, we're beginning to get a pretty good feel for the general approach we need to take. Now, could you get really specific about the actual traits that distinguish the trouble-prone from the trouble-proofed child? Could you gather them all together here so we don't have to search through all this information to find them? Let us know just what traits we need to be developing and which we need to be avoiding."

These are exactly the right questions and at just the right time. I imagine that they have also crossed your mind.

The list that follows is not presented as a complete set of characteristics, but it covers the twenty-four major areas that appear to be among the most important. Experience has shown them to be a nearly perfect predictor of whether or not a young child is likely to become trouble-prone or trouble-proofed. As such, the list provides useful information about where to begin in helping the already trouble-prone children and adolescents. One use I have been exploring recently, is as a part of pre-marital counseling. It helps the couple understand the risks or strengths they will pass on to their own children if those children model the couple's current values.

Please don't assume that these traits are being presented in any special order, as if from most to least important, because for any given child one or another or a group of several may be crucial in his or her particular situation. The form of the presentation here may seem a bit monotonous, but I have found this to be the clearest, simplest, and most straightforward approach. I will first present the trouble prone trait and then the alternative trait that typically leads to a trouble-proofed child. So, with that background, let's begin.

The first trouble-prone trait is represented by a strong tendency to settle disputes through physical aggression. This ranks near the top of the list of reasons that teenagers are called to the attention of both school principals and the police. The trouble-proofed alternative is verbal discussion or thoughtful, logical problem-solving techniques. The healthy, trouble-proofed youngster will certainly care enough about his own well-being to defend himself physically when attacked, but physical aggression is never among his first thoughts when the solution to a problem is needed. Homes that model physical aggression are practically guaranteed to produce children who choose violent, trouble-prone, solutions. Homes that model information-seeking, and logical, problem solving, techniques come closer to ensuring a trouble-proofed approach.

The next trouble-prone trait is a competitive need to at win any cost. The trouble-proofed trait is using cooperative efforts to reach a goal. This is not to suggest that all competition is wrong or harmful, but it does point out that the trouble-prone child rarely, if ever, tries cooperation as a first approach. He believes that winning means he must prove himself to be the best or the toughest or to be able to get the better of someone else. To the trouble-proofed child, winning means the best solution was obtained for everyone who is involved, and it really doesn't matter who specifically gets credit for it.

Some people would point out that the greatest achievements of mankind and of our country have come about through competition. I would not disagree with that. I would most certainly add that by and large the most corrupt and devastating ills of mankind have also been brought about through the fiercest kinds of self-serving, people hurting, competition. The trouble-proofed child's sense of competition will always flow from, and be based on, the eight tenets of the good and humane life, which I presented earlier. When competition doesn't fit within those positive guidelines, it is not a socially, healthful, variety of competition. This concept often takes the most re-education of our adult thinking because throughout our lives we have been taught that competition was fine, right and almost synonymous with The American Way. I urge you to reevaluate that kind of thinking and to categorize competitive undertakings into its useful and harmful forms.

The next trouble-prone trait is to seek immediate gratification - to need to obtain what one wants immediately and not be able to wait for it. The trouble-proofed trait is its opposite - the ability to delay gratification - the ability to plan ahead, save for, and look forward to working toward some goal as yet out in the future. In general, in today's society, the phrase, "I'm looking forward to", has been replaced by, "I can't wait 'til." This new approach does little to teach patience, while doing a great deal to promote impatience and dissatisfaction. It tricks people into believing that if they don't have something they want right now, they are supposed to be unhappy about it. The trouble-proofed child believes that if something is truly worth having, it is worth planning for, saving for, looking forward to, and waiting for. He has learned to truly enjoy the anticipation of some future event or acquisition. The trouble-prone child can't make plans that require a delay into the future. Instead, he just goes out and takes it from someone who already has it, or when older, uses credit unwisely to obtain it legally, or allows himself to get depressed or otherwise distraught because he doesn't, at that moment, have all that he wants. Modeling by the parents is the single most important factor in tipping the scales one way or the other for the child in this important area.

A related trouble-prone trait is to irresponsibly spend and use credit while the trouble-proofed trait is to save and pay as you go. It won't take you more than a minute to recall someone you know who found himself in big money trouble from overextending his use of credit cards. Then, there is that acquaintance or relative who never has enough money to get himself through the month because he spends irresponsibly in an unbudgeted manner immediately after receiving his paycheck. It is a set of traits taught almost solely from modeling the adults in one's life and giving in to the trouble-prone trait just discussed - the inability to delay gratification. The trouble-proofed child learns that he wants to budget, to save, and to plan responsibly. He also must learn that sometimes we do just go without, when legitimate and responsible ways of obtaining something aren't available.

Another trouble-prone trait is lack of respect for other people's property. The trouble-proofed trait is respect for all people's property, including one's own. The child who genuinely respects all property will never turn up in the list of local vandals or thieves will he? He will also take care of his own possessions because he has learned, through carefully planned parental guidance, that things just don't get replaced solely because the child is irresponsible and loses or breaks them. When a child is only allowed to have a limited number of things, such as toys and clothes and treats, he learns to appreciate what he has - to respect his property. Then, he can understand how precious other people's property must be to them, also, and he therefore respects their right to maintain and possess their own things - he respects their property. Children who are allowed to obtain every toy advertised on TV and see every movie and buy every cereal and fill their closet with every new style of jeans and shoes, have no reason to gain a sense of how precious individual things can be. They are doomed to be trouble prone. Children who plan for, work for, and save for what they want most certainly do gain a sense of how precious each thing truly is. Never get caught up in giving things to your children in order to make them like you. First and foremost, you must be their parent and instructor. Their good adjustment later in life will more than make up for their short-lived objections today.

Another trouble-prone, trait is disregard for life itself. The trouble-proofed trait is reverence and respect for life as a precious, treasured, gift. The trouble-proofed child seldom commits suicide or risks taking the life of anyone else - certainly never in a premeditated way or as part of a crime. First, of course, one must truly believe that his own life is precious and a thing to be treasured, protected, and carefully developed to the limits of its positive possibilities. So many children, especially those of the inner cities these days, do not feel this way about their own life. Life seems hard and hurt-filled and something to be endured rather than enjoyed. So, what's the big deal if they get themselves killed - that will only put an end to their misery? And if they feel that indifferent about their own life what reason would they possibly have to feel anyone else's life was any more valuable than that? They have no reason to think twice about killing someone during a robbery or, in fact, just because someone gave them an unacceptable look.

From the time the mother knows she is pregnant it is essential to begin telling the child how precious he or she is. This gets the adults in the right habit, so by the time the youngster is born, our whole approach to him is one that says, "You are precious and loved and wonder-filled." We convince a child of the preciousness of his life in many ways. It can be the tone of our voice, the speed with which we attend to his needs, the tenderness of our touch, the amount of positive attention we give to him, the way we listen to what is on his mind, the way we always answer his questions, the way we support his efforts to gain new skills or knowledge, the way we expect him to be able to follow the rules, our tolerance when he makes mistakes. Treat a child in these ways and he gains the basis for a trouble-proofed life - a life he treasures and respects. In essence, he says to himself, "Any being that is cared for this well, just has to be mighty important!"

The next trouble-prone trait is deceit or dishonesty. The trouble-proofed alternative trait is fair treatment and honesty in all one's dealings with others. We spoke about many aspects of this one earlier as we discussed the trustworthiness tenet. Again, youngsters who get into trouble with the law and with their peers and at school, rank very high in the deceit and dishonesty trait and very low in the fair treatment and honesty trait. It only makes sense! Both traits are primarily learned from modeling those around them - both parents and the older children in their life. It is never a favor to a child to let him get away with deceitful or dishonest behavior. They must be helped to learn, early in life, that these are always prohibited approaches when dealing with others. Believe me, it is easier to teach the honesty trait at the level of cookie stealing than waiting until things have escalated to car stealing.

A closely related characteristic is found in the trouble-prone trait of taking whatever one wants whenever one has the power or cunning to do so. The trouble-proofed trait is to earn, deserve or bargain fairly for what one wants. Taking, in this sense, means out and out robbery, doesn't it? Earning means being industrious, diligent, hardworking - all traits that have helped build America and other great nations throughout the proudest moments of history. Taking also includes accepting the dole or the handout or the government check when there are actually other acceptable means by which one could be constructively supporting himself or herself. To take such handouts when there are alternative ways to make a living is, in my opinion at least, nothing short of outright thievery - a corrupt kind of embezzlement that takes from and hurts the rest of our citizens who work hard to support such programs. Understand that I have no problem whatsoever in supporting any person who is truly in need and to do so for as long as they actually need assistance.

It seems to me that the current-day, materialistic, values have destroyed much of the work ethic that led us to America's greatness. Let me relate a short story. Loretta is the single mother of two children. (1995) On welfare, she could make $950 a month. At the clerical job she holds, she brings home about $750 a month.   Loretta wouldn't even consider the welfare approach because she and her children can live on what she can earn. All of their necessities are covered, and she feels so proud of herself for being able to support her family. Her feeling of pride and accomplishment and doing the fair and right thing is far more important to her than having a few extra dollars each month. It's not that she couldn't put those extra dollars to good use. She could. But she doesn't think it is the right and moral thing to do. In my opinion, we need a whole lot more Loretta's in our World. I respect and admire her so very much, but even far more important than that, Loretta respects and admires herself! Will her modeling help build two trouble-proofed kids? You bet it will!

Another trouble-prone trait is what I call law slipping, that is, paying attention to those laws with which one agrees but not to the others - just letting those others slip by. Exceeding the speed limit when a patrolman is not in sight, is a simple example of law slipping. Tossing the gum wrapper onto the sidewalk is another. Robbing little old ladies on dark streets is a more extreme example of exactly the same concept. The trouble-proofed alternative is law abiding behavior and working to change any laws which seem unreasonable or out of date. Can you imagine how much money we would save as a city or county or state or nation if we didn't have to worry about paying for law enforcement, because everyone valued law abiding behavior so completely that laws were just never broken? Can you imagine the good uses that your budget and mine could find for that money we would save in the taxes we pay! Do children who value law-abiding behavior get themselves into trouble with the law or school officials or Mom and Dad? Do children who value law-slipping behavior get themselves into trouble with the law or school officials or Mom and Dad?

Once again, it is almost entirely the adult and older child models that establish one or the other of these values within the younger child's belief system. Law abiding behavior has to be consistently demonstrated as an always and forever and under all conditions value, or else it is a meaningless model. Which value does she model when the child hears the following explanation from mother: "I believe that we should always obey the speed limit, but today we will be late if I don't exceed it a little bit." The model is totally that of endorsing law-slipping because law abiding is an all or nothing kind of concept. It tells the child that being on time is more important than being a law-abiding person who lives up to his stated personal values. When there is a difference, children believe what they see over what they hear.

Another trouble-prone trait is leadership through physical power - often referred to as dictatorial or strong-arm approaches.

The trouble-proofed alternative trait is leadership through shared power as in a democracy. Now, in the home, Mom and Dad have to be the ultimate power figures and in a way that is a type of dictatorial approach. The essential point here is that as a child matures and becomes capable of learning to make responsible decisions in certain areas of his own life, the parents begin letting him practice doing so. Gradually, as the child matures, he needs to practice making more and more of his own decisions while Mom and Dad are still around to help him pick up the pieces when things don't go right - and never with an "I told you so," of course. By the time a child is eighteen or so and leaves home we want him to be so well practiced in making his own decisions and in taking care of himself that he never again really needs us. We hope he will want us, just not need us.

Shared power comes about gradually within the home. Some aspects of life such as which movie the family rents or where they go on vacation can become early items for practicing the shared power concept. Dictatorial homes that never move toward shared power as the children become capable of practicing it produce children who not only believe they should be the dictator to others but have absolutely no practical practice in how to administer power. In our society, dictatorial approaches stifle growth and participation by others. Democratic, shared power approaches encourage growth and participation of all those who are concerned and capable. Street bullies, gang leaders, and older siblings who beat on younger ones, represent the young dictators. Club members, student government participants, and volunteers represent the youngsters who believe in shared power.

A particularly bothersome trouble-prone, trait is believing that one knows what is right or wrong absolutely without any doubt whatsoever. This usually means that whatever method is necessary to achieve one's goals is thereby thought to be acceptable. For example, Maggie knows absolutely what is right on some subject such as abortion or capital punishment or religious belief. If Joseph believes in a way that Maggie absolutely knows is wrong, Maggie feels it is wholly acceptable to find ways of punishing Joseph for his beliefs or forcing him to come to believe the "right" way - Maggie's way. This leads to societies that are swallowed up by fear and terrorized by these self-righteous know-it-alls who would insist that we must all believe the way they do or face their wrath and rage. It is contrary to the very concept of individual freedom on which our country was founded.

Without a doubt, the line between what should be tolerated and what must be prohibited or curtailed for the good of the society as a whole, sometimes becomes very difficult to define with complete confidence. I happen to believe that those who have learned the alternative trait have a far better chance of protecting our rights and leading us toward growth, as a species.

The trouble-proofed alternative trait is positive value-based open mindedness, in which the way we go about attaining some goal must also always meet one's values and beliefs every bit as well as the goal itself. This one is a bit complicated, but it will become clearer as we go along. At this point just don't mistakenly interpret what I have said to mean that is it bad to think that you know what is right and wrong. I believe that knowing right from wrong is at the heart of any positive value system. I am just saying that when we let ourselves become so closed minded that we cannot even listen to or consider another possibility, or will not allow some other belief to exist alongside ours, we are going to build walls of fear, based on ignorance, between us and others. That is always the most dangerous kind of social situation. You have read history.

I have an acquaintance who in most all ways is a very fine human being. He does, however, hold the belief that a certain kind of person is totally wicked and ungodly so must be punished in every way possible. He spends his weekends harassing and demeaning and stalking these people and, in every way, possible making their lives miserable. On occasion, he has even done bodily harm to some of them. He feels totally justified in behaving as he does, since in his heart he knows absolutely that he is right, and they are wrong. Therefore, these terrible methods he uses against them - methods he would never approve as tactics for use against anyone else - he sees as fully justified and, "approved by God," as he has said. Since on every side of virtually any topic of life there is a group somewhere that believes they are right and the rest of us are wrong, it seems reasonable that such absolute belief systems can do nothing other than destroy us all. I am terrified by those who know without any doubt and without any room for discussion or compassion, that they are absolutely right and therefore have the right to whip the rest of us into line. Absolutists are always trouble-prone people, especially as youngsters. People who are open-minded and compassionate are more likely to be trouble-proofed, especially as adults.

Another trouble-prone trait is simpleminded, straight forward, selfishness. The trouble-proofed alternative trait is altruism in which we are able to often put another person's needs ahead of our own. This altruistic approach builds caring, appreciative social groups that protect one another, as contrasted to the self-indulgent, lawless social groups spawned by the selfish trouble-prone belief.

Young children are, by nature, self-centered, but as they grow, they gain the potential to become less selfish and eventually, as young adults, consistently altruistic. This doesn't mean a person should never put his own needs first. We all need to take care of our own needs - it is the first law of physical and mental health - but most situations call for a solution in which the needs of others, as well as our own, must be considered. Selfish kids take what they want, say what they want, and do what they want regardless of how any of that may affect anyone else. That is definitely a trouble-prone kid who no one will like or want to be around and who will soon be a very sad youngster, as well. Children who are in the process of becoming altruistic individuals are able to think about making other people happy, taking care of them in times of need or sorrow, and allowing others some latitude in meeting their own needs first, even if that means that satisfying one's personal needs must be delayed for a time. Parents, who cannot, lovingly, put their children's needs first, typically raise trouble-prone kids.

A particularly frightening trouble-prone trait is uninformed decision-making that relies on mere opinion, folklore or self-defensive maneuvering. The trouble-proofed, alternative, trait is accurately informed decision making based on a search for reliable knowledge. I have discussed this one at some length earlier so won't pursue the point here. Suffice it to say that the style of the decision-maker model in the home is all-important. A model who seeks all of the pertinent information first, before making decisions or giving answers or administering discipline, helps build the positive value side of this issue and helps the child along the road to trouble-proofing. The model who ignores the facts or doesn't even seek to hear them or find them in the first place, or who makes decisions solely for the purpose of making himself look good, provides the necessary influences to push a youngster toward a trouble-prone decision making style.

Another trouble-prone trait is seeking happiness through materialism - the belief that accumulating bunches and bunches of stuff will automatically give rise to happiness. It never works. Shall I say that again? OK. It NEVER works. The trouble-proofed alternative trait is seeking happiness through integrity, which just means that having a set of positive, socially helpful values, and living up to them each and every day, is the only route to deep down, forever and ever, inner happiness. Kids who believe they have to have all of the newest stuff to be happy, will inevitably end up disappointed with life, because no matter how far their toy boxes overflow into their room, they will just never seem to have enough to bring them happiness. Kids, who understand that happiness stems from knowing they are good and helpful and capable human beings, are well on their way not only to being trouble-proofed, but to living a fantastically happy and rewarding life as well. I understand that in a materialistic world such ours, this becomes a difficult concept to convey to one's children. Demonstrate how well it works for you and you will get converts in the long run.

Another trouble-prone trait is playing Monday morning quarterback - always looking back and deciding how one should have done something instead of dealing with how he actually did it. The trouble-proofed alternative is careful planning ahead. The SAFE technique considers these alternatives, doesn't it? One philosophy can be stated this way, "So, what's the worst that can happen? Surely it can't be all that bad." I don't hear any planning in that one, do you? They then do their thing and the next day look back on it to see how well it turned out. That is a very dangerous approach to life. Another philosophy asks, "What steps can we take ahead of time to be pretty sure this plan will work." Some would say this latter approach is no fun - that it takes all of the surprises and spontaneity out of life. Well, if one wants to spontaneously fall off the cliff or spontaneously get tangled in the underwater weeds when diving off the gravel pit cliff, or spontaneously get caught by the police after tripping the alarm during the grocery store robbery, than, yes, it does prevent some degree of spontaneity. There is, however one undeniable, time-proven fact. Successful adults and trouble-proofed kids, all take careful steps to plan ahead and consider the possible outcomes. Unsuccessful adults and trouble-prone kids seldom even consider that such steps *could* be taken. Perhaps it is sometimes a trade-off between spontaneity and safety. However, it's hard to continue living a spontaneous life once you've fallen off the cliff onto the rocks below or find yourself doing fifty years to life.

Another trouble-prone trait is relying only on peer confidants - having only age mates on which to depend for counsel and advice. The trouble-proofed alternative trait is to have several *trustworthy and wise* adults on whom to rely for such assistance. Perhaps at any age the worst advisor one could choose would be someone his own age. Why? Because someone else your own age may tend to see things slanted in the same general way you do. As one gets older, however, this becomes less of a problem because wisdom and historic perspective can be brought into play. Neither of these traits - wisdom, nor having learned well from ones past successes and failures - is typically present in the counsel from other youngsters or teens.

Wisdom comes with age, which time has not yet allowed the other teen to have. The related and important past experiences necessarily needed for solving one teen's current problems usually have not yet occurred for the would-be teen counselor. There are exceptions, of course. Untrained, peer, counseling, is frequently nothing more than the dangerous sharing of ignorance and misinformation.

Parents who encourage their children to talk with them, by always being willing to listen to them and help them find answers, without confronting them and pointing out to the youngsters how dumb they seem, will continue to be looked to for advice as the child matures. The truly wise parent, however, encourages their children to cultivate other safe, adult friendships outside of the home. Frequently, teens normally feel more comfortable and less threatened when they are talking with someone other than their own parent. Since the adolescent will most assuredly seek outside advice from some source, it is well to make sure you have informally made such good and wise adult counsel available. Teenagers aren't stupid. They know adults are wiser than their friends, but when such a trusted adult isn't available, they will turn to whomever is available. When that is another teenager who knows no more about life than your child does, the quality of the advice and the decisions made as a result of it may be devastating.

The seventeenth, trouble-prone, trait is being willing to be known as a somebody at any cost. The trouble-proofed alternative trait is to need to be known only by one's good reputation. If it takes making oneself into a bully or a fighter or even a killer to be seen as somebody special, then that is exactly what many trouble-prone children will do. They have not been privileged to learn that being known as one with a good reputation is also a way of becoming a somebody. Often their culture thinks and teaches just the opposite. A good reputation means you are weak. A frightening reputation means you are strong.

It is a difficult belief to change so long as the youngster continues to be exposed to that same thinking from his friends day after day. Modeling at home helps a bit, but modeling from the peers is extremely powerful. Begin early and see that the child has the opportunity for friendships of a positive kind - perhaps at a boy's or girl's club, a church youth organization, scouting, a good job setting, time away from the local poor influence by frequent trips to relatives or friends. I fully understand that in some situations none of these things may be easy to arrange or may they even be possible. If the most a parent can do is to require behavior in the home that suggests a positive reputation, then do just that. Keep your own reputation as spotless as possible even if the child may put it down from time to time. Stick by your beliefs and in the long run it should all make the kind of impression you have wanted. Let the child know each and every day that you believe he is somebody really important and that he never has to engage in macho, he-man, or otherwise outlandish behaviors to prove his worth to you.

A related, trouble-prone trait is, continually having to try to prove one's worth, day after day. It usually arises in those who have serious doubts about their own worth. The trouble-proofed trait is, knowing without any doubt that one is a worthy being, so he never has to prove it to anyone else. This comes about through all of the positive methods we have been discussing, so I won't go into more detail here.

Another trouble-prone trait is being inconsiderate toward others. The trouble-proofed alternate trait is being kindhearted. Inconsiderate people have fewer friends and soon get the idea they are, for some reason, less likeable than many other people. The few friends they may acquire are typically inconsiderate unlikable people as well. They then often feel the need to prove their worth or importance in other, inappropriate, attention-getting ways. In most situations the kindhearted youngster is liked, accepted, and is treated nicely by others in return. He feels good about himself and never has to do stupid, dangerous things to prove anything about himself. In some neighborhoods, of course, kindhearted is seen as sign of weakness by some of the peers. Those bullies will have to be dealt with but others who respect the trait are always available.

Another trouble-prone trait is language imprecision. The trouble-proofed alternate is precise language. With few exceptions, trouble-prone kids tend to speak in general terms and use meaningless words and phrases that seldom communicate anything specific either to themselves or anyone else. They use terms such as stuff, things, junk, you know, they say, and punctuate each sentence with equally non-specific or meaningless swear words. In that way, they never say exactly what is bothering them, or specifically what they dislike about certain people or situations or places. Not putting those things into words that carry exact meaning, they cannot possibly regularly think about them in exact ways.

"That blippin' teacher is always givin' us so much blip to do. I hate her blippin' attitude." Exactly what kind of teacher is it that gives this youngster a problem? A blippin' teacher, weren't you listening!! If, instead, he would say that she was inconsiderate, or discourteous, or was one who expects too much, or one who is unfair, or one who is ugly, or one who hates him, then his mind (and ours) would have some actual specific information to think about and to use in helping him to understand himself and his relationships better, or to solve the problem. But when everyone who is seen to be in some way negative is referred to simply as blippin', there isn't much chance for precise thinking or increased personal understanding or personal development. What kind of work does this disliked teacher give him to do? She gives him blip to do. Is that too much work, too difficult work, too easy work, impractical work, or irrelevant work? He has no way of knowing because he doesn't take his thinking that far - he leaves it at the imprecise level of blip. And, of course, not only does his deeper mind not have any idea what he really means, neither do any of us to whom he talks about it. Listeners who really don't care about helping him, will be quite satisfied with his imprecise language because, not really wanting to understand his true problem, they are content to just stay at the imprecise, meaningless level of communication. Those who do want to help either must just continue to feel helpless themselves or must press him to use language that is more precise.

Well, we get the point, I think. Meaningless words such as swear words, all-inclusive words such as things and stuff, and nonspecific personal references such as they, all tend to muddy one's thinking and make clear self-understanding impossible. The child who learns to use specific, precise words and phrases to describe people, feelings, situations, and related experiences, immediately has a means to understand and to evaluate and make plans and develop methods for change. He has to truly understand what he is thinking before he can speak. Then, he hears himself saying what is really occurring. Both of these help him think about things in ways that can be useful. All that the imprecise language user can do is just become more upset in a general way, without having a clue how to proceed to help relieve the actual pain or problem.

Since early language habits are almost entirely acquired from the models at home, parents need to become precise thinkers and speakers. If the children have already picked up such imprecise habits, make a game of restructuring their language with them and demonstrate how, with precise language, the child can actually come to understand himself and others more fully and easily. They can immediately know what is bugging them or what is helping them or what piece of information they need to acquire. Or, if all this blippin blip you've been hearing here, seems to blippin hard, then blip off and close the blippin' book! Got that, you blippin' blipper!

One final observation: People who swear indiscriminately and use other forms of imprecise language, are most unattractive to those of us who want to communicate when we have a conversation. Often, we are the very people who are employers, instructors, supervisors and others who have the power to promote or fire or make life on the job easy or difficult. So you see, precise language pays in more ways than just clearer self-communication.

The next trouble-prone trait is health unawareness. The trouble-proofed alternative is health and fitness awareness. Whether we like to believe it or not, these are the facts. Trouble-prone kids are many times more likely, than trouble-proofed kids, to smoke, drink, use drugs, have sexually transmitted diseases, be either underweight or overweight, have lung disease, and catch colds, flu and other infectious diseases. Trouble-prone kids score significantly more poorly on tests of general nutrition information, physical development information and sexual information. Trouble-prone kids seldom believe scientific or medical information regarding these same topics, while trouble-proofed kids almost always accept such knowledge as true and useful.

Another trouble-prone trait is being an *observation filer*. The trouble-proofed alternative is being a *cause and effect filer*. This is another set of thinking style traits. The observation filer merely watches what goes on around him and remembers - that is files - the images and sounds he experiences. The cause and effect filer not only sees and hears what is out there, but makes the important connections between what causes what to happen or not happen. The cause and effect thinker carefully refer to his file of previous, similar occurrences, so he can then make accurate predictions about what will happen next time, given that same set of circumstances or events. He prefers to have a number of similar cause and effect occurrences on which to base his decision. One just isn't dependable enough. In these ways he can avoid harmful or unhappy cause and effect relationships and he can plan pleasant, happy, safe times.

The observation-filer only carries the memory of what happened and has no sense of why or how to avoid or use that information to his or another's advantage. The closest he can come to using a cause and effect approach is to relate back to the one time before, and one time seldom makes a reliable law of nature or a law of human behavior.

Help children ask questions about how things influence each other and how things come about, and you will be helping to produce a child who thinks like a trouble-proofed, cause and effect filing, kid. Allow your child to merely watch what goes on around him or on the TV and he will become one of the socially handicapped observation filers and will be deficient in one of the most essential skills necessary to keep himself from becoming a trouble-prone youngster.

The next trouble-prone trait is heedless participation. The trouble-proofed alternative is analytic participation. This is, of course, what the SAFE technique is all about, so once again I redirect your attention to that procedure. The heedless participant just jumps into a new activity with no advance consideration of the long-term consequences. The analytic participant hesitates as long as it takes to think through the possible consequences before making a decision about participating.

Another telltale, trouble-prone trait is chaotic or haphazard living style. The trouble-proofed alternative is the purposefully organized living style, with dependable routine and recurring daily benchmarks. At least nine times out of ten, detention home residents come from homes that have no day to day or hour by hour routine or schedule. There are no set times to get up and to go to bed. No set times for breakfast, lunch and dinner. There are no set times to do homework or to have enjoyable times with other family members. These children seldom sit down to a meal as a family.

On the other hand, the vast majority of trouble-proofed children do have set routines in their homes. It seems that even such a minimal routine as eating two meals a day as a family helps a great deal. A schedule helps a child learn about organizing his life. Without this understanding it becomes fairly impossible to get on with such other important aspects of life as planning ahead, setting and working toward goals, fulfilling one's obligations on time (such as getting to work or school on time), and constructing and carrying out other deliberate, planned activities. Life unfolds as a set of unpredictable, chance, occurrences.

This brings us to the final set of characteristics. The set that universally distinguishes the future trouble-prone kid, from the future trouble-proofed child. The trouble-prone trait is an exclusive peer orientation. The trouble-proofed alternative trait is a beneficial combination of peer and family orientation. Children who spend some time with their friends but first of all have a solid relationship with their parents and brothers and sisters, and who spend a significant portion of their non-school and non-job time in their own home, usually become trouble proofed. Those who seldom relate to their other family members and who spend the vast majority of their free time unsupervised, with their age-mates, will become trouble-prone - and you can bet big money on it.

By knowing this one fundamental and incontestable truth, it would seem we should be smart enough to raise trouble-proofed kids, wouldn't you think! Of course, it isn't that simple. I know about some home conditions in which I am sure the child is better off being out on the streets with his friends. This doesn't mean he still won't end up being trouble-prone, but at least he will be alive and perhaps won't be an addict like his mother and brother or have the violent approach to problem solving that his father demonstrates, or rent out his body for sex like his sister.

Chapter Four

It is becoming more and more apparent that substitute support environments can contribute in significant ways to the trouble-proofing of children whose own homes just cannot provide or model the characteristics which I have been discussing. I'm not even speaking about actually removing a child to another home. A substitute support environment may be that Boy's Club down the street or the church basement three nights a week or the recreation program at the school from three to six o'clock each afternoon. It may be that big brother or big sister who takes the child away from his home environment for even as little as three or four hours each week. It may be scouting or bluebirds or 4-H. It may be band or chorus or drama club or the school newspaper staff. It may be sports. It may even be you, sitting on your front steps at three ten each afternoon, making yourself available for Mary as she stops by to have that chat after school before continuing on to her home.

All of these kinds of programs seem to have a major and helpful impact on many children. All potentially trouble-prone kids should probably be absorbed by one or more of these, substitute, support environments. Today there aren't enough to go around.

Since we clearly can't assure each child an adequate, trouble-proofing home environment and neighborhood, I hope we are smart enough to create ways to increase the number of these absolutely essential, substitute support environments.

At this point, it seems essential to spend some time talking about just how people are able to control and influence each other.

How people influence each other

Social influence is a powerful force in all of our lives and yet it always operates on just one very simple, very easily understood, principle. When somebody - or something they offer to us - is able to meet one of our unmet or under-met needs, we tend to be influenced to try what is offered with the hope of satisfying or gratifying that need. Stated more simply still: If you can give me what I want, at a price I can afford, you can influence me.

I was at a park not long ago observing the people there for the very purpose of finding real life, everyday examples of this process. Within the first ten minutes I had jotted down more illustrations than I could ever use - that is how universal this social influence activity is in our lives.

A five-year-old had been dispatched by her mother to retrieve the three-year-old brother who had wandered off. The little girl soon found that tugging on him or trying to carry him did not influence him in the intended direction. Then, I could just see the light bulb go on above her determined young head. She reached into her pocket, pulled out a piece of hard red candy and showed it to the little boy. Then, keeping it just out of his reach she slowly retreated toward her mother with little brother in hot pursuit. She had something that would meet the brother's sweet tooth need so she was able to influence him. Had tugging on him or picking him up, met any of his needs? No. If anything, they went against his normal three-year-old youngster's need for independence. Had his big sister, at this ripe old age of five, already mastered the basic principle of social influence? You bet she had!

Then there were the two fifteen-year-old boys speaking in

somewhat hushed tones behind the tree, in front of which I was sitting. I could watch them in the reflection on the window of a car parked near-by. Their conversation was punctuated with frequent glances toward a girl who lay sunbathing some thirty yards away. "You show her some of this stuff and she'll do anything you want her to - I mean anything, you get my drift?" the first, more worldly looking lad was saying. After a few more longing looks at the scantily clad girl on the Snoopy beach towel, the second boy asked, "How much?" Soon the deal was completed, and the boy was off to try and weave a spell on his female prey. It must have worked, because after a brief session of roll in the grass, suck face, and touchy-feely, they left the park together. The first boy had known which need was always on the mind of a fellow fifteen-year-old male, right? And, whether that translated to the second boy as being able to appear macho to the girl, or sexy, or worldly, or as the provider of a high old time, or as a way to get her into bed, he took the bait and purchased the necessary material. In return, she seemed to have taken his bait, so he must have found a way to meet (or hold the promise of meeting) one or more of her needs.

Finally, there was the eleven-year-old boy who was beating the holy tar out of his nine-year-old brother. The beer-bellied, tank-topped, heavily tattooed father walked up to them, picked up the older boy by the belt, and proceeded to unmercifully slap his face a dozen times or more, all the while yelling profanities at the lad who was soon screaming out in great pain. The boy was then instructed to lay face down on the ground, spread-eagle, and stay there, which he did for over an hour. He was still there when I left - absolutely motionless except for the shallow movements of his abdomen as he sobbed in terror. The older boy had been trying to influence the younger one, hadn't he? In this case, he chose the use of physical pain. Stated in terms of needs, he chose to take away the younger brother's need for safety or physical pleasure, probably promising to give it back when the smaller one modified his behavior in some way or changed his mind about something or just cried Uncle. I only had to wonder for a moment where the older boy had learned that method of influence, since the father almost immediately proceeded to use the same hurtful method - a process I refer to as the restriction of need satisfaction.

Social influence: somebody else making us believe that they can make things better for us, if we will just do as they say. We are bombarded by it all day long on TV and radio and in the newspapers' ad sheets, aren't we? Interestingly, even when we know what those out-in-the-open advertisers are up to, we still often take the bait and buy things we really don't need and didn't even want before they told us we did. The same types of influences are aimed at our children every day from their peers, the other adults in their lives, their music, their heroes, and the whole gambit of the entertainment choices available to them. When they are unaware of how others go about influencing them, they are easy picking for anyone who wants to persuade them. More frightening than that, perhaps, they are profoundly influenced by models out in their world who aren't even trying to persuade them to do anything special or to change them in any special way. The sports star who, acts aggressively, immorally, uses drugs, smokes or drinks, does influence them.

Persuasion proofing

So, what kinds of things can we teach our children that will help persuasion-proof them against all of these subtle, shrewd and powerful influences? I suggest a three-step program. First, help them understand what their normal basic human needs are. Second, help them understand which ways of meeting those needs are safe and acceptable, and which are dangerous and inappropriate. Third, provide ample opportunities for them to meet all of their needs in acceptable ways that are totally in line with your own philosophy of life - the values in which you believe. I would suggest that an essential starting place is to help the youngster evaluate potential need-meeting activities by making sure they are in line with the eight basic tenets of a humane and civilized life, presented earlier.

It is completely amazing to me how so few teenagers can make an accurate list of human needs. When they get beyond food, drink and sex, they seem stumped. Trouble-proofed children always do a far better job at this than do those who are trouble-prone, but it appears that this essential area of self-understanding somehow gets left out of most parents' child-rearing plans. It is also amazing, though reassuring to me, that once trouble-prone teens come to discover and understand their own needs and the alternative ways of meeting them, a great many of these youngsters are able to suddenly turn their lives around forever. [I have to wonder what schools are teaching our children when such basic elements as self-understanding seem to be so often omitted.]

One of the most rewarding and indescribably astounding experiences I get to have is leading value discovery workshops in juvenile detention and teen-addiction rehabilitation centers. When such a session has gone well (after two hours of intensive confrontation, give and take, and sweat and tears), everyone just sits back totally exhausted. Each one is silently reflecting on their possible new outlook on life and is consumed by the knowledge that so much of the hardship and heartache in their lives, and in the lives of those who love them, could have been avoided, if they had just possessed this knowledge a few years earlier.

This, is predictably followed by another hour of anger, hostility, outrage, and ranting and raving, all directed at those people, who earlier in their lives, had been charged with raising them properly, but who had failed to help them understand these several simple, but absolutely important concepts about life. It mostly boils down to the eight tenets already presented and to understanding the following ideas about human needs and how they can be satisfied in ways that are in everybody's best interests.

Human needs

Most persuasion techniques tap into one of only about eight or ten of our basic human needs. We have more, of course, but these seem to be those most easily used. This may be because they are the ones which are most often not being met or are being under-met, that is, not being satisfied fully or often enough.

Food and nourishment represent the first need area, but this one is usually only found to be a good persuasion hook in the very young or in those living in complete poverty. Therefore, I won't say more about it except to point out that trouble-prone children usually know less and care less about nutrition than do trouble-proofed children. Kids also listen to what TV tells them they should want to eat and drink and thereby pick up appalling ideas about nutrition.

The needs for Safety and freedom from threat of harm have always been important but rank close to the top of the list for many inner-city children these days, since their neighborhoods have become so dangerous. To meet this safety need one typically avoids certain potentially harmful places or people or behaves in certain ways so as to not be physically punished - that is hurt or killed. At other times one seeks out the company of certain stronger or more influential people because associating with them may keep you safe from certain hurtful folks who are afraid of such people. When gang membership appears to be the only way to achieve personal safety, then gang membership it is.

There are, or can be, other alternatives, however, in most neighborhoods. It is important to make these other havens available and to show how they provide a positive direction for the child's life compared with the gang which can only maintain the miserable status quo or provide even more dangerous and harmful, no growth, no win, outcomes.

It seems so unjust that providing safety and freedom from pain is so easy in some areas of our country, and so nearly impossible in others. This is an issue for which affected neighborhoods must organize themselves in order to bring about change. It is being accomplished in small pockets all across the nation, so we know it can happen. Local, grass roots leadership and neighborhood courage, seem to be the essential elements. When it comes down to a choice between life itself, and whatever alternative is being presented, that alternative automatically wins out. So, safety must come first, and some realistic alternative means for achieving safety must be found and pointed out and practiced. Trouble-prone children are far more likely to feel they are in danger than are trouble-proofed children.

The need for entertainment is always a good hook for those who are set on persuading us. Entertainment basically means anything promising to break a current state of boredom, and generally takes one of two forms. Either some kind of enjoyable activity or some kind of physical pleasure based on movement, taste, smell, touch, music, or sexual satisfaction. There are dangerous ways of meeting each of these needs and there are safe ways. There are ways that are socially approved and there are ways that will ultimately get one criticized or into trouble. It is a basic responsibility of a parent or a child-caretaker to find ways of making the positive approaches easily available and to seem more appealing, logical, and sensible then the negative ones.

When physical and mental entertainment, such as amusement parks, movies, dances, picnics, club activities, family activities, board games, mental contests, reading, and sporting events aren't available, altered state entertainment, such as tobacco, drugs and alcohol tend to move in. Trouble-prone kids report that they experience boredom and a lack of physical and mental entertainment opportunities to a far greater extent than do trouble-proofed kids. Trouble-prone kids also report little interest in things such as clubs, organized activities, reading, playing sports, family activities, arts, crafts, playing musical instruments, mental activities of any kind, and even watching family type TV programs. Trouble-proofed children report just the opposite. It would appear that trouble-prone children seldom have the chance to experience, practice, and grow to appreciate, those socially acceptable and personal growth producing activities. Since boredom will not be tolerated by most healthy human beings, especially teenagers, altered state entertainment or dangerous - getting a rush from living on the edge activities - are often the only alternatives they see.

Another basic need is status. The trouble-proofed kid feels that either he has an adequate amount of status just because of who and what he is and how well he is living up to his own standards of conduct, or he is willing to seek improved status in socially acceptable ways. The trouble-prone kid typically feels he has no meaningful status to begin with, or that he has gained status purely because he has become one of the bad guys of the World. It may also be that he is seeking to achieve such bad guy status by his current, trouble-prone, behavior.

Kids, and even adults, confuse being respected and being feared. Respect is a positive feeling of status that we have toward someone who represents socially positive standards. We respect the cop who risked his life saving the child from the fire. We respect the parent who worked hard and made an honest success of him or herself. We respect the boy next door who took it upon himself to plant, care for, and harvest a small garden for the crippled old man down the street. We respect the teacher who went way out of his way to help us in our personal life when we needed it so desperately.

Fear, on the other hand, is a feeling we have toward someone who we believe could hurt us in some way if we didn't playthings according to his directives. Producing fear in this way often produces a kind of status, but it is not respect. We fear, rather than respect, the playground bully, and pay up rather than get beaten up. We fear, rather than respect, the gang members and, therefore, we may not testify to the crimes that we have seen them commit. We fear, rather than respect, the parent who rules through physical punishment or verbal abuse. We fear, not respect, the neighborhood drug lord. We fear, not respect, the cop on the beat who turns out to be actively racist. We fear, not respect, the judge who is overly severe or unpredictable with his or her sentences. We fear, not respect, the politician who gets us favors by abusing his power.

Given one's unique set of circumstances, he may set out to be like the hard working, helpful gardener boy or like the playground bully. It depends on what route to status one believes is open to him. We'd all prefer to be respected but, rather than remain a totally unknown nobody, most healthy youngsters will choose, instead, to be feared because that, at least, provides some kind of notice - some degree of status. We have to find alternatives to the status through fear route and provide avenues by which positive respect can be sought and achieved and maintained by all children. Learning to do something well, is the surest way to winning respect - winning the respect of others as well as achieving the all-important self-respect.

The trouble-proofed child can usually tell you the difference between how the bully and the hero obtain their status, and they consistently choose to copy the hero and achieve the respect that can come with it. Just the opposite occurs for trouble-prone youngsters. They have already given up on gaining status in any socially positive way, if in fact they were ever led to consider it in the first place. Their approach is based on schemes to become a bad enough dude so nobody will mess with them, or so they can just take whatever they want. To gain such a reputation usually entails a good deal of hurtful, illegal, socially destructive activity. In many neighborhoods it is next to impossible to even talk with young teens about gaining status in positive ways. In all honesty and with complete sincerity they absolutely cannot conceive of that ever happening for them, and if they believe that it can't possibly happen, what's the chance they will ever even try (or listen to someone trying to suggest such alternatives)? Major changes in those sub-cultures must occur and must occur in the immediate future.

Happily, for most children in our country, exposure to socially positive models and striving to be respected can be bona fide possibilities. We all have this need for status, even if it is only the status we give ourselves privately for living the good life as we have defined it, but we all do need status and (short of debilitating depression or mental illness) we will all find our ways of achieving it.

We all have the need for friendship and interpersonal love. Being a recluse - a total loner - is not a pleasant state of affairs for the vast majority of human beings. Having friends tells us that we are acceptable. It is a wonderful way of proving our worth. Close, dependable friendship becomes an overwhelming need during adolescence - often so strong as to overpower any and all other needs for a period of time. Teens will even regularly risk their personal safety and their long-term health in order to make and keep friends. They will risk their good name and that of their family in order to make and keep friends. They will even go to jail, thereby giving up their personal freedom and their rights to entertainment, fun, social, and sexual pleasures, in order to make and keep friends.

When the peers who are available for a child promise to be a good influence and allow a safe, comfortable, happy existence, parents breathe a major breath of relief. When the opposite is true, we all hold our breath anticipating the worst. In the most extreme cases - neighborhoods in which there just doesn't seem to be a single good kid to be found - other family members then have to become the child's good and trusted and satisfying friends. That will work when it has to. I've seen it happen, many dozens of times. It's not the approach we would wish for, or plan for, but it can work. A better solution might be to find one or two neighborhood children who show some glimmer of positive possibilities. Let them make your home their safe haven - their place away from home in which, with your help, they can grow and share and find friendship and love - a friendly stopover in their otherwise bleak world. In this way you gradually build an acceptable friend for your child - if only for the short run and if only there in your home.

I have known children who had absolutely no concept about what love between family members meant. Not having ever experienced it they could not, of course, seek it, or could they even begin to trust it when it became available. Friendship and love: two extremely important needs. They are the two needs most often used by those who would try to persuade our children along the wrong lines. Friendship and love. The gangs, the cults, the hate groups, and other socially, dangerous subcultures, all promise friendship and total acceptance so long as the individual bows to the beliefs and requirements of the group.

The trouble-proofed child typically has socially positive friendships with both peers and adults and knows without a doubt that he is loved. The trouble-prone child has to seek the satisfaction of his needs for friendship and love in less desirable and more dangerous relationships. It becomes so easy for the unloved adolescent to confuse love with that of any sexual relationship. The language we give them to use – "making love" – even promotes that most dangerous and growth-limiting misconception, doesn't it?

Another need is to have possessions. No one disputes that we all need some things, some stuff in our lives. The dispute comes over which things and how many possessions are necessary or realistic. We've talked about this a bit before - about how some folks tend to seek their happiness by acquiring stuff. ... So, what do we really need? We all need clothing, shelter, educational materials, medical and health related supplies, entertainment devises such as games or TV's perhaps, and possibly a few other things. The persuaders of the World would first try to convince us of how inadequate our present supply of possessions is, and then how having the ones they are promoting will make our lives simply wonderful, now and forever more. (Well, at least until their next new model of that product comes on the market.)

Kids like stuff, don't they? They like new toys, gadgets, games, new clothes and shoes. That's all pretty normal. Kids' minds aren't as able to think abstractly, philosophically, and altruistically as we adults can, so they think in terms of stuff. It is when we have led them to believe that possessions are all important that they become easy prey for the stuff peddlers. The trouble-prone kid worships stuff, plain and simple. He will do whatever it takes to obtain the stuff he is led to believe he needs or that gives him status or that will bring him pleasures or that will make him popular, bright, strong or sexy. Although the normal trouble-proofed kid has most all of those same desires, he keeps them all in a more realistic perspective and knows for sure and certain that his worth as a person has absolutely nothing to do with how much or what brand of stuff he possesses. Most trouble-prone kids feel their worth is indeed almost totally reflected by which stuff they have.

We all have a need for a wise confidant - a counselor, a trusted advisor. Although similar to a friend, this person must also appear to us as exhibiting wisdom. To the four-year-old it is the five-year-old who seems wise and all knowing. To the ten-year-old it is the twelve-year-old. To the trouble-proofed teenager it is a parent, a trustworthy older friend, a teacher, coach, clergyman, or the boss at his part-time job. To the trouble-prone teenager it is his gang leader or another adolescent who possesses no more wisdom than he does. The parents of trouble-proofed teenagers encourage their youngsters to talk with and confide in wise adults outside of the home. They understand how an adolescent who is struggling to gain his parent's respect and earn new freedoms and privileges often can't bring himself to reveal his weaknesses or problems to his parents. In the old days, we had Grandma, Grandpa, Uncle Mike or old Mr. White across the street. Today such trustworthy, wise, third parties are often more difficult to find. They are still essential, however. Remember that one teen's mother is another teen's confidante. Kids will find an advice-giver somewhere. Better it be at home or from a friend's trusted parent, than from Slick Sam the con artist down on the street corner.

This next need is so complex, that if I were to adequately cover it, I would fill a small volume. At adolescence, the need for physical, sexual pleasure becomes an overwhelmingly important need. It has been conservatively estimated that the average, healthy, emotionally stable teenage male thinks about sex at least once every two minutes and dreams about it almost every time he sleeps. And, it would seem that the teenage girl, apparently, isn't all that far behind her male counterpart in the amount of mental attention she gives the subject. Combine this need with the need for tender, intimate friendships, and you have a sure winner.

Adolescent boys and girls seem to approach this sexual area of life quite differently, so perhaps we should be speaking of two separate needs - one for males and one for females. For the boy, a sexual relationship is entered into far more casually than it is for most girls. He approaches it much like he would a game of monopoly with friends. Typically, it is, for him, quite strictly a way to enjoy a female's body and to bring about a relatively rapid sexual climax for himself. Love, friendship, tenderness, and commitment often never even enter his mind, except as useful ingredients in a line that will get him what he wants (needs). For some boys these concepts do genuinely enter their thinking, but most often, they do not. For the girl, the sexual relationship is often a means for obtaining special attention and, hopefully, a degree of tenderness from a male they find physically and personally attractive. Experiencing the intense and ultimate sense of sexual delight usually seems to play a far less important role for the girl. (At least that's what teen girls have told me.)

Often, sexual activity is more truthfully seen as a delight-filled route by which one or more of the teenager's other needs, can be met. Sex is frequently mistaken for fulfilling one's need for interpersonal love. It is typically seen as a form of wonder-filled entertainment - more like a sport, in fact for many teens. For some, it is a means for obtaining friendship, and a sense of belonging to or being extremely important to someone else - perhaps more often for girls than boys. In certain social groups, like gangs, for instance, an ongoing sexual relationship with one strong or influential male, often offers safety for the girl, since her partner will protect her from others and from the ever-present dangers in her neighborhood. Sexual activity, or the boasting thereof, has been an age-old source of status among teenage boys. A continuing sexual relationship with a person of status brings some of that status to their partner- male or female - as well. So, the seeking of sexual pleasure is more often just that - a sexual climax - for the adolescent male, whereas for the female it is very often coupled to the achieving of some other need or needs as well. This is not an absolute rule, of course, but my experience with teens would suggest these are reasonable and justified generalizations. So, now, how do we use this knowledge?

Most parents and adults hope (and teach) that teens will delay sexual activity with a partner, either until marriage or until they are considered adults under the law. Some go so far as to teach that even sexual pleasures one induces on himself - that is masturbation - are to be strictly and totally avoided. These are burning issues in many quarters, and I won't go into my personal position here. I will relay the fact that any impartial search of man's history shows, almost universally, that cultures in which interpersonal sex was absolutely restricted just to marriage partners, have produced strong, long-lasting marriages and continuing family units that generally raised law-abiding, well-adjusted children. Those cultures in which casual, non-committal sexual activity was permitted or encouraged, have seen the all-important family unit virtually disappear and have produced generation after generation of criminally inclined and maladjusted offspring. There have been a few exceptions, of course. This is not a legitimate topic to answer according to one's opinion. It must be answered on the basis of fact, so I encourage you to conduct your own search of the history books.

The final need I will discuss is the need for integrity. Integrity literally means completeness, and that is essentially what I mean when I use the word. Integrity infers completeness between one's positive value system and the way one actually behaves. Other synonyms for integrity are morality, honesty, virtue, and uprightness. Well, you get the idea. It is my contention that this state of integrity between one's positive belief system and the way one actually lives one's life is the essential element in achieving deep down, life long, inner happiness.

My experience with many thousands of children demonstrates beyond any shadow of a doubt to me that, every day, the trouble-proofed child actually thinks about this connection between what he believes is right and how he acts. The same experience tells me, over and over again, that in the first place, the trouble-prone child has no clear concept of what constitutes socially acceptable behavior. In the second, he seldom if ever thinks about evaluating his own behavior to see if he is living up to some such a positive, socially beneficial standard. When the trouble-proofed child gets into a scrape he feels bad that he failed to live up to what he knows is right. In the same situation, the trouble-prone child feels bad that he was so dumb as to allow himself to get caught. Integrity: the single most important human need, if mankind is to survive as a species.

How the persuaders of the World use these

normal needs to a youngster's disadvantage.

People meet their needs either by moving toward something in order to achieve it, or by moving away from something in order to avoid it. We tend to move toward that which gives us pleasure or satisfaction or provides growth, and away from those things that either appear likely to harm us in some way, appear to be too difficult for us to achieve, or merely hold no interest for us. Often there is some cost involved in order to escape from the unpleasant or the boring, or in order to acquire that which we are seeking. That cost may be in money, effort, compromise, risk, danger, or any of several other commodities in which we humans trade. We each have to decide if the price, whatever it may be, is justified and reasonable to us at that moment. We have to compare that price with the price of other experiences that will allow us to achieve the same (or a similar) goal. Typically, the trouble-prone child fails to do this - does not look beyond the offer of the moment - never seeking safer or less expensive alternatives.

The drug dealer approaches a ten-year-old boy for the first time. They chat about a lot of things not related to drugs. The dealer learns that Jerry seems to always be striving for something new and different - that he enjoys new experiences. The dealer's approach with him, then, is that he has something that Jerry can take, which will give him a wonderful new experience like he has never ever dreamed he could have. ... This same dealer approaches Bobby for the first time. Bobby, come to find out, is very unhappy with his home and school and friends and even himself, and tries to find things that will help him get away from all of that. So, in this case the perceptive dealer promises that this very same stuff he has will make Bobby's cares disappear and that he won't even have to think about all those problems so long as he uses it.

Jerry was a youngster who moved toward things in order to meet his needs. Bobby moved away from things to meet his needs. Either way, this dealer, well versed in the ways of human need fulfillment and motivation, knew just what to present to each, didn't he - approach new and wonderful experiences for Jerry, and escape from painful, troublesome experiences for Bobby.

Even though the first bag of pills to each boy was going to be provided free of charge, Jerry knew even that price was way too high, because he had been provided with adequate information about drugs and addiction and how dealers approach youngsters. Bobby, on the other hand, even having heard that there were some big risks, thought he had little to lose, and would have gladly paid hard cash for that first, free, sack. At the time of that meeting, Jerry was on his way to after school intramural basketball and, fortunately, for him, that met his needs for excitement and new experiences just fine at that crucial moment in his life. He also had other interests in music and reading and scouting, and family activities. It seemed utterly senseless to

Jerry that anyone would ever consider using drugs to try to achieve what he already had naturally. Bobby participated in no activities or sports and hated being around his punishing, degrading family. At that crucial moment in his life he had nothing special to do, so this chance to escape the boredom and pain of his existence seemed to hold grand possibilities.

Bobby's mother couldn't understand why her son was so intent on getting into drugs, that is, she only saw him as moving toward drugs. She missed the whole point that he was actually moving away from his life. Whenever we see a youngster apparently moving toward something that is obviously known by him to be harmful or dangerous, we must search for the opposite side of the coin - what is it that he is actually moving away from?

Beth's mother was concerned because Beth wanted to spend less and less time at home and more and more time with her friends. The mother's question was this: "What's wrong with things in our home that Beth needs to avoid us here?" Again, this is a one-sided view. Flip that coin also and ask if, as a normal twelve-year-old, perhaps she is not actually fleeing from home but just moving toward new and normally important peer relationships.

So, the bottom line, here, goes something like this. When a child moves toward something that appears to us to be harmful, we have to stop and determine why the child sees it as positive, since he will only move toward that which he feels will offer some positive experience or alternative to his present circumstances. We must also ask what need the child is trying to meet and how could it be met in some safer, more positive, way.

The art of making suggestions to children and adolescents

How can we provide that better way without appearing to be forcing the child to accept it. Remember, especially with an adolescent but also with any headstrong child, *force from a parent always results in the parent losing*. The child may also lose, of course, but either way, things are made worse instead of better. The adolescent always needs a face-saving way out of a problem or a rapidly deteriorating position. It must be one that always looks like he - and no one else - is the one making the mature decision.

We drop hints, we make subtle suggestions, we ask leading questions, and then swiftly leave the topic before the youngster can state a position that opposes our own. Never get into a situation with a teenager in which he is forced to take a stand against what he needs to be considering or doing. The useful techniques are variously referred to as hit-and-run or, my term, Seeping the Deep Mind. Both mean the same thing. We open up an area for the youngster to consider without ever forcing the idea or trying to convince him of its worth. Any teen of even low average intelligence can take the ball from the point of first encountering a new idea and then considering and working with it all by himself. If, later on, he wants to talk about it, fine, but at that point always remember it has become his idea and not yours.

Often, adolescents, who typically find it difficult to admit their ignorance or lack of sophistication - especially to their parents - can't bring themselves to ask a question that might seem to put them in such a bad light. So, they make some brazen, bold, seemingly ridiculous statement and then sit back and listen to the parent's response until they hear the answer to the question they really wanted to ask in the first place.

Jack comes home one night, plops down on the couch and announces to his parents, "I don't think there should be any laws against teenage drinking. It's just a big stupid deal invented by adults who want to keep the good stuff all for themselves." What *question* do the adequately prepared parents hear? They hear him asking for opinions and legitimate reasons why teens should not drink and to make sure he understands his own parent's position on the subject. In this case, Jack's parents can carefully provide all of that information without ever letting on they realize he is asking these apparently uncomfortable questions.

In a similar situation, Mary's parents rant and rave and belittle her for her ideas and threaten to ground her until she is thirty if she ever touches a drop of the filthy stuff. Although the experience is terribly unpleasant, Mary does get some, though by no means all, of the answers she was seeking. Her parents just didn't understand about this normal, teenager's data gathering process. In fact, their emotional reaction suggests that they took it as a personal affront - an attack on their personal belief system.

How soon we forget! It's hard to believe that most all of us were also once young experts at using that method, and yet we often have such a hard time recognizing it for what it is when we see it being used, today, by the teens in our lives. We need to remember and smile to ourselves when we see it happening, and then methodically and concisely provide whatever information we think they may actually be wanting. At least they came to you. Keep it all short and sweet. Never repeat yourself during such a monologue and state each point in as few words as possible to make the point. And just how will we know when we have finally supplied the data the youngster was seeking? When they storm out of the room, of course!

I don't mean to imply that some adolescents aren't still able to sit down calmly with one or both parents and ask the important questions that are on their minds. Many can, and these are truly wonderful moments because they imply a very special kind of trust and respect. They suggest trust in the parents' desire to understand and in their ability to accept and love the youngster even if he or she isn't perfect (doesn't know all the answers). They suggest respect for the parents' opinions, values, knowledge and wisdom. These moments, of course, come easier and more frequently when they represent a natural extension of a life-long series of such serious, calm, positive discussions about matters of concern to the child.

Let's summarize

Let's stop at this point and summarize the major elements we have shared here in the last few sections of the Trouble Proofing program. Bringing them together will make it more convenient for you to take notes if you choose to do that. I believe it is a fine idea. Reading it all is one thing but putting it down, so you actually see it in your own writing, and making your own handy reference guide makes a lot of sense to me.

I listed and discussed a number of traits that almost always differentiate the trouble-proofed from the trouble-prone youngster. Let me list those again, leading each time with the trouble-proofed characteristic. As you read them this time, think of them as positive and negative values - ways of thinking, believing and behaving that become basic principles by which one directs their life.

Trouble-proofed (positive)
rather than
Trouble-prone (negative)

Logical problem-solving techniques
    rather than
    physical aggression

Cooperative
Rather than
an unbridled competitive approach

Ability to delay gratification
rather than
the need for immediate gratification

A save and pay as you go approach
rather than
irresponsible spend & credit approach

Respect for all property
rather than
lack of respect for others' property

Reverence and respect for life
rather than

disregard for life

Fair treatment and honesty
rather than
deceit and dishonesty

Earning what you need and want,
rather than
merely taking it

Law-abiding behavior
rather than
law-slipping behavior

Democratic approach
 rather than
 dictatorial, strong-arm approach

Positive value-based open mindedness
rather than
belief in absolute right and wrong

Altruism
rather than
selfishness

Accurately informed decision making
rather than
uninformed or lore-based decision making

Finding happiness through integrity
rather than
seeking it through stuff, status, or power

Planning ahead
rather than
Monday morning quarter-backing

Having adult confidantes
rather than
only having peer confidantes

Being known by ones good reputation
rather than trying to be known as
a somebody at any cost

Knowing one is a worthy being
rather than
having to keep trying to prove one
is a worthy being

Kind-hearted
rather than
inconsiderate or otherwise hurtful

A user of precise language
rather than
imprecise language

Health and fitness awareness

rather than
health unawareness

Cause and effect filer
rather than
an observation filer

Analytic participation
rather than
heedless participation

Purposefully organized living style
rather than chaotic/haphazard living style

Peer *plus* family social orientation
rather than
peer-only social orientation

Then, I suggested this definition of social influence: When someone or something they offer to us is able to meet one of our unmet or under-met needs, we tend to be influenced to try what is offered, in order to satisfy or gratify that need. Stated more simply still: If you can give me what I want, at a price I can afford (or fool myself into thinking I can afford), you can influence me.

I talked about moving toward that which we think will meet one of our needs and moving away from anything that would appear to be threatening one of our needs, and how influence peddlers use these two approaches to hook us into their sales pitch.

Then, I listed these basic needs which often play a part when we are being socially influenced or persuaded. Food and nourishment; Safety and freedom from threat of harm; Entertainment, which can take one of three forms - physical, mental or altered state. Another need is that of Status, and I spoke of the difference between gaining it through fear or respect. There are friendship and love. Then, there is the need for stuff, and I spoke about necessary vs. excess stuff and about the uselessness of searching for happiness in bunches of stuff. Then there is the basic human need to have a wise confidant or counselor. We spoke about the need for sexual pleasure and specifically how it applies to the adolescent years. Finally, we spoke about the need for integrity and how the survival of mankind may well be based on having all of us achieve Integrity - living up to our highest, positive, socially beneficial, standards.

I then spoke a bit about two differing approaches to making suggestions to strong-minded children and to all adolescents. I suggested that the confrontational approach should typically be avoided, and how methods such as face-saving techniques and Seeping the Deep Mind usually work best with the older youngsters.

Finally, I talked about the usefulness of the adolescent's big negative statement technique. That occurs when they make some outrageous proposal and then sit back and listen to the adult's responses. I suggested that this is a normal alternative for them to asking a question outright, particularly when they are afraid such a question might make them look foolish or dumb or ill prepared for the next privilege they hope the parents will bestow on them.

Chapter Five

Problem solving techniques

Many years ago, a very unhappy woman told me that her main problem in life was that she always felt so frustrated. For years she had fretted and fumed, and sought help in numerous places, always focusing on her overwhelming feeling of frustration - being determined that was her problem. As we talked, and after much discussion and logical sparring, she ultimately came to see that being frustrated is never the problem. What she should have been doing all those years, was to ask what was making her feel so frustrated, and in finding that answer she would discover the actual problem. Feelings of frustration are never the problem. A problem always lies behind a frustration. Find that problem and solve it and the feelings of frustration vanish.

That story is a prelude to presenting the first step in problem solving. How do we know that a problem exists? We know on one of two levels. Like the woman in the story, there is the hidden level, in which we feel anxiety, fear or frustration, but can't attach it to anything specific. Problems at the hidden level may require a good deal of exploration and even specialized help to discover. Such problems are often uncovered by asking questions like:

115

"What about my life is not the way I want it to be, or is not heading in the direction I had always planned that it would be?"

"How am I not living up to the picture I have had of myself?"

"Who or what in my life might I be reluctant to face as being or making a problem for me?"

"What things about my life do others point out to me as being problems that I just may be unreasonably disregarding?"

Once the source of a hidden problem is established, much of the uneasiness usually disappears immediately because you finally know what it is all about. Then, it is just a matter of applying some good problem-solving techniques.

The second level we can refer to as the obvious level. This category includes those problems that are right out in the open. Problems with relationships, activities, goals and values, motivation, and all other hurdles or obstacles that we confront on a day to day basis. These are easier to discover and to begin working on than are those at the hidden level. If one knows that he never has enough money to get through a week that is a pretty obvious problem. The necessary solution is equally as obvious - either he makes more money, or he cuts his expenses. He then asks himself, "How can I accomplish one or both of these things?"

Here is another example. A teenager wants to be on the basketball team but, year after year, he gets cut from the squad before the season gets underway. The problem may be obvious, or it may be hidden. We begin by asking what about being on the team appeals to him? Is it that he likes to play basketball? If that's the case, there are pick-up games on every playground at virtually any hour of any day. Is it, perhaps, that he wants the status that he thinks will come from being on the team? If so, it appears he is going to have to discover other ways of achieving the status he needs. What other avenues could be open to him? Does he need that team membership because he thinks it is a way to get a scholarship for college, which is one of his longer-term goals? If so, it's time to search out some other financial aid sources.

So, again, how do we know when a problem exists? Either it is so obvious that we can't miss it or we feel so uneasy that we know something is not the way it needs to be even though we can't immediately put our finger on it. Young children's problems are usually of the obvious type - "I lost my socks," "Bobby is hitting me," "I don't understand the assignment," "The new baby is taking too much of your time, Mom." But even young children may have hidden problems. "I feel angry since the new baby came into our home, but I don't know why?" "I wonder why I'm no good," asked a six-year-old who had jumped to this conclusion when she noticed her mother didn't ever hold her while she spent lots of time holding her new brother.

As children mature, those who have open relationships with their parents, who can ask them their important questions and expect reasonable, immediate answers, seldom develop many hidden problems. Those who don't have such a relationship, often do. A father once outlined to me his conception of his family's current and overwhelming problem in this way: "Garrett is simply a six-year-old brat. He won't mind. He destroys things. He will never wait his turn. He is so impatient. He interrupts constantly." All of that made this, quiet, attentive, little boy there in my office appear like a monster, or like a hyperactive child with an attention deficit disorder, which was, in fact, his father's personal armchair diagnosis. Was it any wonder the child chose to sit alone in a chair across the room from his parents?

Come to find out, in this home the questions that Garrett asked were never answered. He never had first choice at anything. His parents never initiated conversation with him because they were too involved with each other. They filled the house with their own precious nick-knacks and would seldom buy the boy things such as a bike or books or toys when he asked for them. Their reasoning was that they didn't think he'd take care of them.

Garrett, as it turned out, was by far the sanest member of the family - he wasn't about to be ignored, was he. He was most definitely going to demand the attention and care that was his right as a child, as a human being, and as a family member. One Monday evening I outlined to that family what I felt was the real problem - a problem, which to Garrett, was of the obvious variety but to the parents was of the hidden type. A new family relationship plan was developed on Tuesday, and by the following

Monday the father had nothing but praise and affection for Garrett, who, on this occasion, with a smile from ear to ear, spent the entire hour in my office cuddled quietly on his father's lap. These intelligent adults, who hadn't the slightest idea of how to be parents at an emotional level, were able to quickly turn things around once they obtained the necessary information. They had always loved their son but were, for several reasons that we won't go into here, unable to initiate an appropriate relationship with him. Many years later I had occasion to watch, then fifteen-year-old Garrett, openly give his mother a lingering hug and kiss as he got out of the car in the school parking lot. How about that for a problem solved!

The point here isn't that I'm such a fantastic therapist or teacher, but that once the real problem is defined, solutions often - in fact usually - come rapidly. Such a large proportion of folks seem to wrongly define their problem - they insist it is one thing when it is actually something quite different. The bottom line, then, is that you can't solve your problem until you are quite certain you are working on the actual problem.

On a related topic, let's take a few paragraphs to distinguish between worrying and problem solving. Worrying involves replaying the problem or unpleasant event(s) over and over again and thinking about the dire consequences that are sure to follow because of the problem.

"I'm always broke at the end of the month so my children will go hungry, the utilities will get cut off, and we'll freeze to death, huddled in a corner of the bedroom."

Well, perhaps this seems a bit exaggerated, but it is an actual problem as once presented to me by a single mother. But what was the mother doing - problem solving or worrying? Worrying, of course. How did it benefit her or her children? It didn't, in fact it took up all the time she could have been using to create a solution. Worrying is the number one method people use to avoid having to get started on the solution of a problem.

Each day we all meet problems that we must solve. Some are easily solved if we will just get organized and do it. Some are solved with far more difficulty and need more planning and careful attention. A few we may not be able to solve at all.

A fourteen-year-old boy listed the following four problems as the reasons for his anger and depression:

My parents are divorced.

I hate my sister.

I'm failing algebra.

I think I'm a sex pervert because I masturbate all the time.

First, we separated these into two lists - those he had major control over and those he had very little control over. In the "I have control over list" he placed algebra and masturbation. In the "I have no control over list" he placed divorce and his hated sister. We later transferred sister to the other list. Ten minutes of discussion and fact giving about his sexual fears, banished them forever, and he even marked it off the page because it was no longer a problem. This was a case where just having appropriate knowledge about a subject handled the problem. Mere lack of appropriate knowledge is a frequent source of problems, especially in children and adolescents. It also contributes to many parenting problems.

As we discussed the algebra problem it came out that he had been assigned to a tutor for help but hadn't been going because he was so bummed over being a pervert. Once he no longer feared that, he was eager to begin attending tutoring and since he knew he wasn't dumb he decided that would no longer have to be a problem. He temporarily eased things between himself and his sister by deciding that for his part he'd stop teasing her as punishment for being someone he hated. (Yes, as soon as he heard himself say that, it all seemed quite stupid to him, also.)

That left the divorce, which he came to understand was something over which he had no power. He began devising ways to live with it and ways to reduce the anger he felt toward both parents for doing this to him. We arranged several one on one discussions between him and each parent, in which he asked them a number of very pointed questions that he had prepared ahead of time - questions about the divorce that had been quietly bothering him for years. That eventually cleared up his own guilt that had grown out of his belief that he had somehow caused it all to happen. A pleasant and useful relationship was eventually reestablished between him and each of his parents. He even came to accept and enjoy his father's new wife.

He had been so intent on reversing the divorce and on hating his sister that he had not been able to see that some of the other problems could be easily solved. Once they had been handled his depression lifted and he found new emotional energy and time to use in dealing with the other problems. As he became more mentally efficient, he soon got a good grip on life. As he put it the last time I saw him, "The best thing about all this, Doc, is that I learned how to separate problems into three types: those I can solve, those I can handle, and those I have to live with. Now, I'll be able to do that for myself all the rest of my life." This is what we want for our children, isn't it - for them to be able to gain the skills that will stay with them and help them for the rest of their lives.

Help them list their problems in order from those that they think will probably be the easiest to solve to the most difficult, and then help them get started on eliminating the easy ones while they continue to think about ways of attacking the harder ones. Every time one is solved, they have that much less frustration or fear in their life and that much more energy to put toward tackling the others. Then, if after all is said and done, one or two unsolvable problems remain they have a clearer mind, increased self-confidence, and more energy to use in finding ways to handle and live with or around those situations.

My son loved to play basketball and was actually very good at it. One-on-one he took on and outplayed each of the first-string players at his high school. One problem! My son was only five feet seven and the first strings in that league averaged well over six three. In a game situation, he just couldn't compete. It was one of those unsolvables so long as he remained determined that the only solution was to play first string basketball.

When he accepted the reality of the situation - the inheriting of short genes from Mom's side of the family - he was able to create several alternatives with which to handle the problem. He volunteered as a coach at the boy's club. He formed an intramural team at school, which he carefully selected to be composed of fine players who, if they had not been ineligible for some reason, would have made the team, and they walked off with the school championship three years running. Did he get to continue playing basketball? Did he play on a winning team? Did he find a way to gain some status as a knowledgeable basketball player from the younger kids at the boy's club? By having risked going one on one with each of the first stringers had he gained both his own and their respect as a competent player? Was he later on able to look back at his school basketball career in a positive way? He had found ways to solve those parts of the problem that could be solved, and ways to live with those that couldn't? (He was a remarkable young man.)

He and I were both so pleased that he had never learned to just be a worrier or a fretter or an escaper when faced with a challenge but had developed the necessary confidence and problem-solving skills to keep after such things. And, oh yes, I would be remiss if I didn't also relate that he found a way to solve one additional basketball related problem. His senior year he came to me on the afternoon before the championship intramural game and quite openly, directly, and authoritatively said, "Pop, please don't make an exuberant ass of yourself at the game tonight!" You may rest assured that I was the best-behaved beast of burden in the entire gym that evening.

Let me now pull all of what I have been saying into a simple problem-solving system. It is so simple, in fact, that you must not blink, or you may miss it. There are seven parts and you will want to come back later and copy them down in your notebook.

First, determine if the problem you are considering is occurring at the hidden or at the obvious level.

Second, make certain that you are, in fact, working on the real problem. Approach this through open-minded consideration on your part and through discussions with others who know you pretty well.

Third, make a list of all, or at least most, of the problems that seem to be bugging you.

Fourth, rewrite the list, in order, from the one that seems easiest to solve to the one that seems likely to be the most difficult. An alternative to such a list is to group all the problems into the three categories: easy, moderate and hard.

Fifth, begin the actual solution of the easiest ones while continuing to give some thought to how you might go about working on the others. (This is just the opposite from the way in which most poor problem solvers approach their problems. They often feel they must solve the ones that bother them the most, first.)

Sixth, when your list is down to the few most difficult ones, determine if they can or can't be solved at that point in your life. If they can, go to it. If they can't, you will need to begin designing ways to live with them and stop fooling yourself into thinking that someday soon it will just all go away. Face it. Handle it. Relax about it. If all of this still leaves you anxious or depressed, seek professional help.

Seventh, as new problems arise from day to day - as they will, of course - add them at the appropriate levels in that list. Remember that at the outset I said this wasn't intended as a 'problem-proofing' program. We all have problems to solve. Those children who learn how to solve them, are quite likely to become trouble proofed. Those who just choose not to deal with their problems, as well as those who are poor problem solvers, most definitely, become trouble prone.

One final comment about problems. Problems help us grow! Without problems to solve, and challenges to overcome, human beings deteriorate as thinkers, as survivors, and in their ability to help others. Children who get to practice solving problems for themselves get so good at it that later on when Mom and Dad are no longer handy, they can do it all by themselves. I have known dozens of college freshmen who had previously had all of their problems solved for them by Mom and Dad. Not having acquired the know-how to take care of themselves, they rapidly became unhappy, frightened, desperate and failing young people during that first semester away from home. It is never a favor to a child to shield him from his own real problems.

For as far back as I can remember I have always appreciated a good problem because it gives me a chance to feel vital and to accomplish something new and wonder filled. It makes me realize that I am stretching my limits as this human being that I am. The problem with problems is not that they exist, but with the fears and ineffective methods with which we approach them.

So, I urge you to eagerly accept a problem for what it is - an opportunity for you to discover something new and useful, to grow, to remain vital and mentally alert, and, perhaps, to make a useful contribution to the knowledge of mankind. Get your children involved early in this problem-solving process. As small children, when their own skills at problem solving will still be rather inadequate, be sure they at least come to understand that they need not be afraid of problems. By always taking the necessary time to assist them in finding adequate solutions you will help them come to understand that their problems can and will be solved. This will encourage them to want to learn how it is done.

Later on, teach them the seven specific steps in approaching problems and help them as they practice. As in any other skill, problem solving takes practice, guidance, and much trial and error groping. Kids need our support as they struggle to become successful at this most important skill. If, at first, they stumble and even fail in their attempts that's just fine, because you will be there to calmly help. When their problem-solving attempts fail we always give them credit for trying and then help them discover how to improve their approach. Help them look for more than just two sides to each issue, in this case to each problem, and answers will come more and more easily.

So, trouble-proofed kids are not problem-proofed kids. They are however problem-identifying kids, problem-analyzing kids, and problem-solving kids. Too often trouble-prone kids are problem avoiding kids who are far more adept at finding ways to escape from a problem than at even considering that it may, in fact, have a solution.

Problems between people: Arguing, discussing and debating

Arguing, discussing, debating, and problem solving are four entirely different processes, although they are often mistaken for one another. Each one leads to very different end results, because each one has a very different purpose. So, when the one selected isn't right for the situation at hand, problems usually become even worse.

A discussion is a learning process in which people share facts or ideas on some topic of mutual interest. It may also involve talking about the likely results of several different possible solutions to a problem, though the purpose of a discussion is not to select a solution; it is to provide all the important related facts and information. The people involved in a discussion are not trying to influence each other to a certain point of view – they are pooling information and isolating important, related, questions.

Arguing is often wrongly thought to be an informal type of debate. In a debate, each of two sides of an issue are presented by two speakers, in an attempt to convince the third person (the listener) to accept one of the two points of view. For example, two politicians debate on television in order to each present their positions, each one hoping to persuade voters to vote for him.

In an argument there are usually two people, each trying to win the other (rather than someone else) over to their own way of thinking. In most cases neither of the arguers has any intention of changing his own belief, so arguments never really end and most certainly never solve anything. Studies show us quite convincingly that once an argument begins, each person automatically begins believing in his own position even more strongly than he did before. It is called defensive reinforcement and just means that once someone begins defending his side of a disagreement, his belief in that position becomes harder and harder to give up. It is as if each time one takes his turn to speak in an argument, he adds a big block of stone to the wall growing up between his ideas and the other person's ideas. Arguers seldom really listen much while the other one is talking. Instead, they use that downtime to think up new ways to support their own position. It is a talk, search inside, talk approach, rather than a more useful talk, listen to the other, then respond to what they said approach.

In problem solving, the goal is not just to present all the necessary facts, like in a discussion - though that is an important part of problem solving. And, arguing, since it never ends or solves anything, is never a part of this problem-solving process. There are, of course, many different kinds of problems. Let's focus for a moment on disputes between people. There are several steps that must be taken to solve inter-personal disputes.

First, agree on what the dispute really is, and state it clearly - better yet, write it down so there can be no doubt between the parties about what it is. Keep to just one specific topic at a time. Many times, once the actual problem is agreed on, the parties involved can find a solution immediately. I remember a couple of teenagers who had argued most of the night and, of course, had not solved a thing. Come to find out, the boy was arguing that he wanted more time to himself away from his girlfriend, and she was arguing that when they were together, she wanted them to do more of the things she enjoyed doing. Since they had not taken the time to state the problem, they rambled on arguing meaninglessly in different directions for six hours. After they had the chance to clearly state the problem about which each one was concerned the solutions (to the TWO problems) came within five minutes. You might be surprised just how often this kind of misunderstanding about the actual problem topic, really occurs.

The second step is this. As you are talking, and before you add your next statement or respond to the one just made by the other speaker, make sure you fully understand what the other person means by what he just said. The other speaker must agree that you have re-stated his idea accurately before you move on and make your next addition to the conversation. Example: Mary says: "Your mother always seems uncomfortable when I'm at your house." Bill restated what he thought he heard Mary say in this way: "You think my mom hates you." Of course, that was not at all what Mary said, was it? What if the argument went on without first getting that straight? They would each be arguing about a different topic wouldn't they - Mary about an uncomfortable mom, and Bill about a mom accused of being a hater of Mary. It is easy to see that when the two people aren't talking about the same topic, they can't possibly find a solution. Please note that it is never appropriate to argue over what the other speaker really meant by what he or she said. You MUST accept whatever they say they meant as the truth. For instance, Bill wouldn't be allowed to argue that Mary may have used the word "uncomfortable," but that she really meant, "hated." If Mary says "uncomfortable," then "uncomfortable" it must be.

This leads us to the third step. You must agree on word and phrase definitions. Make certain that you both mean exactly the same thing by the words and terms you use. In the phrase: "You always laugh at me when I skate," what does the term 'always' really mean to each party? Does it mean every single time, or does it mean often? Does it mean once in a while, or perhaps, something else entirely? Never assume that you both define every word in exactly the same way. The fact is, we all have our own little personal interpretations attached to most terms. SO, ask and find out. And, don't argue over whose definition is really correct - each is really correct for the person using it. Just find out what they mean and then go on with the problem-solving mission. In the Mary and Bill example, there would be several more words to clearly define, wouldn't there - uncomfortable and hate, for two.

So, if you want to make sure that the other person never gives up his original position on a topic, by all means, argue with him - that's guaranteed to keep him from ever changing his mind! If you want to learn as much as possible about some topic or about what someone else thinks about some topic, then discuss it with that person or with someone who knows a lot about it. If you want to persuade groups of people to think as you do, then find someone who thinks differently than you do and debate the issue in front of them, so those other people can decide for themselves whose ideas make the most sense.

But, if you want to solve a dispute or a difference of opinion between you and someone else, use the interpersonal problem-solving approach. Begin by using these three basic steps: (1) Agree on the exact problem you are discussing. (2) Make sure after every single statement that you understand exactly and can restate accurately what the other person meant by what he said (without any argument about it). (3) Be certain that both of you are defining key words or terms in the very same way. By using just these three simple techniques you will speed toward helpful solutions to the disagreements that come up between you and anyone else.

A few more hints about child-rearing

Sprinkled throughout the discussion so far have been many suggestions - do's and don'ts if you will - related to child-rearing techniques for those parents who are seeking ways of raising trouble-proofed kids. There are several more which I believe are essential to our discussion, but which haven't fallen neatly into any of those previous presentations.

The first is what is usually called consistency. Normally, healthy, well-adjusted children will all push the limits and try the rules once in a while just to make certain that they are still there - that they still understand what the family boundaries and expectations are. When the child finds that Mom and Dad stick to what they have stated as being the rules and expectations, the child can draw a breath of relief, knowing he still understands things correctly. He may not like some of what he finds out, but at least he has discovered it is all still just as he remembered it to be. It is consistent.

If, when he tries the limits, Mom or Dad gives in or doesn't enforce a previously stated rule, then the child has reason to become anxious and unsure and distressed. Why? Because he discovers that somehow the rules of life were changed, and he wasn't informed about it. That is plenty of reason for the child to suddenly become very angry. Parents have often commented to me that they weren't able to understand how their child could be so unappreciative when they were given some special privilege. In no time at all, they tell me, the child was out of control. The reason? Inconsistency. The rule was changed and although the child was willing to take advantage of it if it were to his benefit, the anxiety still built up and soon gave way to anger.

It is even more difficult for the child when the next time he tries to push that same limit he finds that it is back to being enforced again. We call this inconsistency and it is one of the major causes of mental illness in children. In the least, it virtually always produces a trouble-prone kid. Giving in or temporarily turning off a rule is quite confusing to the child. It makes him mistrust all the rules at home as well as question those out in the big world. So, a rule should either always be there or never be there.   Anything in between promises most unpleasant consequences. This highlights how very important it is for parents to put a lot of serious thought into the careful construction of their rules.

When a child senses that a discrepancy may exist between what he thought the rule was and how it may be now, the normal child will continue to test it until he is satisfied that he understands what the current state of affairs really is. We have all heard, and probably even used, the expression, "Give that kid an inch and he takes a mile." That saying could be called the age-old law of inconsistency, because it outlines exactly what I have been describing. The problem with it, as stated above, is that it seems to blame the child who takes the mile, rather than the adult who inconsistently gives the inch, that is, who temporarily changes the rule or the limit or the expectation. When we have a good reason to modify a rule temporarily, we must make certain that the child fully understands that the change is only temporary and that he will be clearly notified when it reverts back to the old way. For example, when on a vacation, things such as bedtimes or snack times may be altered or some of the expected jobs may be eliminated or changed. Then, when vacation is over, it must be clearly back to the old routine again.

Younger children - those ages five and under - have a very difficult time with the concept of temporary. To them, once a requirement or routine is changed it is changed for ever and ever no matter what you say, so it is always best to keep their routines and rules and expectations completely consistent. It just isn't doing them a favor, or even being nice to them, to complicate their lives by giving in even once in a while.

There are certain benchmark times in a child's life when

rules and expectations do change. As children become more mature, they gain new privileges and, also, the associated new responsibilities. The parent's expectations change. Bedtimes change. Where they are allowed to go, changes. Who they can be with, changes. What they are expected or allowed to wear, changes.

These should be wonderful times both for the parents and for the child. The parents recognize that they have been doing such a good job as teachers and models that the child has grown sufficiently that he can be trusted to take more responsibility for some of his own decisions. The child is pleased to have received the new privileges and new freedoms. The essential element related to our discussion of consistency is just to make certain that you formally sit down with the child and go over the changes and what they mean, and state exactly what the new setup is to be. Have the child tell back to you what you have told him so there is no basis for doubt in any discussions that may follow. Once the new arrangements are thoughtfully made, we don't take them away. It is then our job to help the child learn to live up to them. We expect there will be some problems and errors in judgment. After all, that is how we learn and grow, and eventually become wise. Isn't it?

This next topic is difficult to name. I sometimes refer to it by this long, awkward phrase: "I will do what I think is right for you without regard for whether it will make me popular with you or not." Let me explain further.

One of the surest ways to create a trouble-prone kid is to only do to or for him, those things that you know will make him like you. The responsibility of the parent is, I believe, to do to or for the child those things that will help him grow into a responsible, likeable, happy, socially beneficial, human being. Along the road to achieving all of this there will be many times that what he needs to experience will not be what he wants to experience at that moment. When we force the issue - as we must do - we can fully expect to be less than popular with him for a while.

When I was about four, I suppose, I took a sugar cookie from a neighbor lady - one I had not been offered - and hid it in my shirt until I got home. Mom discovered it and marched me right back to return the cookie and to apologize to the lady. I remember wondering how my Mom could possibly hate me so much that she would make me do that frightening and humiliating thing. I stayed terribly angry with her for all of, oh, I don't know, seven minutes, perhaps. Had she instead, said, "Oh, it's ok this time – I'll even cover for you - but you must not do those kinds of things again," what would I, as a four-year-old, have heard? I would have heard that it's really ok to do what I had just done, because that, remember, is how the four-year-old would normally think - temporary means permanent. I would have liked Mom a whole lot more at that moment, but I certainly would have learned the wrong lesson about life and therefore, perhaps, liked her a lot less in the long run.

I have known many parents who make parenting into a popularity contest, thinking they must keep the child liking them at all cost. It is a particularly common state of affairs in cases of divorce, where the parents are vying for the child's loyalty and love and affection, or where, by making it seem the child loves them the most, they can thereby bestow additional pain and anguish on the ex-spouse. What a terrible way to harm an innocent child using him to meet one's own very sick, revenge-filled, needs.

There is a law of parent-child relationships that goes like this.

"The parent, who *thoughtfully and appropriately* does to and for the child those things which need to be done, giving no particular thought about whether it will make him more or less popular with the child, will, *in the long run*, have gained the respect of the child."

It is long, but so very important. We all would like to have our children like us, of course, but there are times when we must be able to delay that particular form of self-gratification and instead just go ahead and do that unpopular thing that needs to be done. When, later on, the grown child understands why we did what we did, and sees how that helped, you will have his respect.

Some children learn early on that once a parent has disciplined him, very soon, that parent will be back doing something extra nice for him - as if making up for the discipline in order to keep in the good graces of the child. Some children even work this to their own advantage, misbehaving on purpose so as to get that special something later on. The momentary discipline of the parent is easy pre-payment for the "goodie" to come. This, of course, is not how things need to be, is it.

Up to now, I have talked all around this next topic without, perhaps, stating it specifically. The topic is discipline and what it means and how it is achieved. In general, it is a most misunderstood term. The dictionary supplies us with two basic definitions for the word discipline:

First: Ability to follow a set of rules and regulations, like the well-disciplined athlete.

Second: Training that develops self-control, like learning to hold one's anger in check.

When I ask parents to write down their own definitions of discipline, the overwhelming response is Punishment. Now, punishment is one of the several methods long used by parents, attempting to help children learn to follow a set of rules and regulations, and to help them develop self-control. But it is only one method, and just plain and simply is not what is meant by the larger concept, discipline. Punishment is a behavior control method, but it is most certainly not discipline.

One of our goals for children is the development of self-control or self-discipline, isn't it? Developing the ability to live by a set of socially beneficial rules or values without having to be forced to do so, represents self-discipline. Down through history there have really only been three main behavior control methods.

First: Parents who see misbehavior as a deliberate bad force set somewhere deep inside the child, may try to punish the child severely enough to keep that force from ever getting loose again.

Second: Parents who see misbehavior as just not understanding how to get along in positive ways, tend to spend a lot of time rewarding good behavior and ignoring bad behavior. The theory is, that behavior, which is rewarded will continue and that behavior, which is ignored will, for lack of attention, eventually fall by the wayside.

Third: Parents who see misbehavior as faulty problem solving, put time and effort into helping children acquire effective problem-solving techniques, so they will be able to keep themselves from making those same behavioral mistakes again, thus being able to help themselves behave appropriately anywhere and anytime.

Children raised by the first method - punishment - often become trouble-prone. Virtually all trouble-prone children have indeed either been raised by the punishment approach or have had no consistent training approach used at all. Children raised by the reward approach and the problem-solving approach, typically are not trouble prone. However, when the positive rewards stop, many children who have been raised solely under that approach become confused and fall apart, apparently needing to have some agent, like a parent, on hand to continue doling out the rewards, letting them know when they are doing ok.

Children raised by the problem-solving technique, combined with the rewarding of good behavior approach, tend to be far less trouble-prone than most, and, in fact, almost always become trouble-proofed, provided their belief system (values) is a socially helpful one. I emphasize the positive values here, because good problem-solving skills can also be acquired by children who possess a socially destructive value system - those who have learned that to be a destroyer of others or a user of others is the appropriate way of life. They, of course, are trouble-prone kids, but may well get away with their offensive behavior a bit longer, because of their good problem-solving skills.

In light of this, perhaps we should add as a Fourth behavior control method: instilling positive, socially beneficial values in the child. This becomes the most effective control system later in life, even though it may not be able to play a fully effective system in the child.

One more comment, here, about the reward system. Some behaviors just cannot be ignored because they are injurious or harmful to someone. Those must be stopped. It is the less dangerous, negative, or useless behaviors that are rapidly eliminated by being ignored and by making certain that they generate no reward - no positive attention - from the misbehaver's point of view. (Most parenting books explain this more fully.)

So, begin thinking about discipline as a positive, useful, state of mind we want the child to achieve - an end result - self-control - rather than as a method of helping a child conform to the rules. When the training method is consistent; when it is based on the belief in a socially beneficial set of values (such as the eight tenets); when it uses rewards or positive recognition for desired behaviors and ignores non-injurious types of undesired behavior; and when it emphasizes effective problem solving techniques; you are almost guaranteed a trouble-proofed child. You just may want to go back and copy down that entire last statement.

Building decisive human beings

Most of us admire people who can be immediately decisive - that is, people who can make high quality, accurate decisions quickly, with no hem-hawing around. We certainly want our children to be able to make high quality, accurate decisions about all-important personal matters. When they can do so quickly, all the better, especially out in the World where it seems that a danger of some kind may be lurking around most every corner. Why can some kids do this, and others cannot? The answer, believe it or not, is quite simple. Decisive folks know, without any doubt, what their personal rules of life are. When something comes up out in the world, they simply refer to that set of rules. If the proposal or opportunity or activity fits those beliefs in an acceptable way he says, "Sure, let's do it." If it doesn't seem to fit, he says, "No way. I'm out of here."

So the secret to making quality, instantaneous decisions - that is to be able to be one of those admired, decisive people - is to know without any doubt what you believe so you can quickly act on those beliefs. Teenagers who possess a positive value system and also have this ability to be immediately decisive will typically be trouble proofed. Teenagers who either do not have the capacity to be decisive or are decisive but base those decisions on a negative, socially non-helpful set of values will, without any doubt, be trouble-prone kids.

Priorities

When all is said and done, trouble proofing comes down to a set of priorities. The dictionary tells us that: "Priorities are those several special beliefs, activities, or possessions that are felt to be more important than most others."

So, if we were to each list all of the things that are important to us and do so in the order from most to least important, we would have an ordered list of our priorities. By glancing at your list anyone could immediately know which things would rank as important goals for you and which would be less important. They could predict which kinds of things you would select or do when given a choice or when presented with a dilemma. Priorities about things reflect our preferred lifestyle. Priorities involving values and behaviors, translate into how our personality comes across to others.

Think for a moment or so about how people holding these two contrasting sets of priorities would go about their respective lives.

Person A:
1. car
2. house
3. money
4. promotions at work
5. family

Person B:
1. family life
2. charity/volunteer work
3. self-improvement
4. work
5. money

Paint a picture for yourself of each person. How does each of those sets of priorities tend to affect the world that person lives in?

A quick glance at a person's budget is another fine way to get a good idea about his priorities. Think about where the most and the least money is budgeted. Is if for the car, dwelling, clothes, vacations, furnishings or other possessions, time payments, things for the adults in the home, things for children, charity, savings, books, club memberships, education, church, political donations, drugs, cigarettes, alcohol - well, the list could go on and on, but those should make the point.

I like to differentiate between two kinds of priorities. I call the first superficial or surface priorities, and the second, fundamental priorities. How are they different? Suppose you made a list of your twenty-five top priorities, as suggested above, ranked from most important to least important. These represent the superficial priorities. Then, for some reason you had to get rid of all but six of them. Those six were the only ones you could have from that moment on for the rest of your life. These represent the fundamental priorities. Which priorities would you keep from your list? Those relating to family or money? Entertainment or education? New cars or charity? Politics or savings? And so on. When doing this exercise some folks find that many of the possession or status-oriented priorities are given up in favor of things like happiness, integrity, family relationships, health, world peace, education, and other more socially positive pursuits. That first list of the superficial priorities may or may not have the fundamental entries highly ranked. When one's fundamental priorities are socially positive, a person is far more likely to be living a socially useful life and feel the basic sense of integrity that I suggest is the only true route to deep down personal happiness.

Another, perhaps less complicated, way to think about these two concepts is this. You are to be left on a small tropical island for the next five years, totally isolated from anyone or anything you do not take with you. Food and water are provided for you there. You are allowed to take ten things with you. These could be anything but might, for example, include a car (with ample gas), a stereo, a spouse, a child, books, TV, clothes, money, happiness, self-esteem - virtually anything or any feeling or anyone. What would your list include? These things would indicate your fundamental priorities - those things which, above all else in life, are the very most precious to you.

I have suggested a host of values, behaviors, goals, and procedures that need to rank among a parent's highest priorities if their child is to have that absolutely vital opportunity to become trouble proofed. In turn, the child must then accept, for himself, that same system of priorities if he or she is to become a trouble-proofed youngster.

The parental model is all-important when it comes to setting such priorities. When the child sees a set of priorities working to provide deep down inner happiness and personal fulfillment for his parents, he is eager to embrace it as his own. When he hears one set of positive priorities being preached by his parents but sees them living by a very different set he is confused and doubt ridden. He realizes that if his parents don't believe in their stated priorities enough to live by them that there must be something fishy going on. Sad though it may be, perhaps one step better than living with that kind of inconsistency, is for the child to see a parent living by a set of priorities that obviously makes that parent and family miserable. That way he may at least be able to see what things to eliminate from his own priority list.

Here is a general test by which one might judge each item in his or her priority list. Will it help lead to, or at least be compatible with, a safe, healthy World, in which everyone can respect, trust, nurture, and encourage positive growth in all human beings? A "yes" allows it to remain on the list. A "no" requires one to consider removing it.

This is not as restrictive as it may sound. It doesn't actually require vows of poverty or saintly goals. It even allows some selfish goals and behaviors, after all, we are each, one of those humans mentioned in the test question, and as we said earlier, if we don't take adequate care of ourselves, we will be in no condition to assist others.

That test statement allows for all of our basic human needs to be met and most certainly promotes joy, happiness, and satisfying entertainment and leisure time activities. It encourages the development of our creative side. It requires that one's work activities be socially helpful and therefore allows us to live a moral and ethical life on the job as well as off. It restricts the goals of competition to those having mutually helpful and socially desirable ends. In these ways it guides us each toward the place where our behavior is totally in line with the way we believe about what is right and what is wrong. This state I have referred to as integrity, and I believe it is the highest state of human development.

More specifically it requires us to live by the eight essential basic philosophic tenets presented earlier, or by some other, comparable, socially positive set of values. It requires us to be faithful to our daily mental tune-up so that our priorities continue to be the ultimate guiding forces in our lives. It requires that we teach our children specific techniques, such as the SAFE technique, ways of looking for all possible options, and proven problem-solving methods, in order for them to properly evaluate and react to their World. It requires that we help our children value accurate knowledge and learn to depend on and cherish fact over unfounded opinion or folklore. It requires that we strive to incorporate into our lifestyle and philosophy those characteristics that prepare a youngster to be trouble-proofed rather than those leading to the trouble-prone life.

It requires us to help our children understand how methods of persuasion operate and how to make high quality decisions in the face of them. It requires us to help our children fully understand all of their natural human needs and to find realistic and acceptable ways for meeting all of them. It requires us to seek out and master those child-rearing techniques that have been shown, down through the ages, to move children gently and positively toward our priorities. Such things would include learning the appropriate ways to approach and talk with children and adolescents, parental consistency, useful and long-lasting approaches to discipline, and methods for helping youngsters come to love and value themselves as precious beings.

Let's summarize

We have just covered many important pieces of information. They are so important I want to carefully review them with you.

We discussed problems and problem-solving techniques.

How do we know when a problem exists? We know at the hidden level when we feel anxious or frustrated but can't pinpoint the cause. We know at the obvious level when the problem is out in the open. But we must be certain that what we think is our problem, actually is the problem. Sometimes it is helpful to determine if some trusted friend agrees with our definition or description of one or more of our problems before we set out to solve it.

Young children's problems are usually out in the open. By age seven or so they may begin feeling anxiety about the hidden variety as well.

When preparing to attack your several problems so you can get on with life, free from so much strain and stress, begin by just listing them. Then put them in order from the one that looks easiest to solve to the most difficult one. Or just place them into one of three categories: Easy, moderate, or hardest. Then get to work on the easiest ones while continuing to think about ways of attacking the more difficult ones. Sorted out and approached one at a time they will seem solvable, so you are more likely to get to work on them. Examined all at once, as one big jumble, they may just seem overwhelming, forcing you to avoid them or run away from them or deny that they exist. Look for many sides to each issue - search for many possible solutions even after you find one or two that seem useful.

Some problems will not have solutions, so you have to find ways to live with or around them. Some of these, however, may only actually be unsolvable at the moment. In such cases you will need to patiently wait for some period of time to pass before you can really do anything about them. Examples include the teen with acne and the child who relates best to adults (he'll eventually be one, so things should be better then).

Each day or as needed, add to your list those new problems that arise. Place them at the appropriate level of difficulty. Attack them in order along with the others.

Try to think of these problems not as your enemies but as your friends - as opportunities to grow and learn new things about the world or other people or yourself. Problems truly can help us feel vital and mentally alert and may provide one with that wonderful chance to make some awesome contribution that will benefit mankind. Without problems to solve, which thereby force us to grow, human beings would shrivel up mentally and become like vegetables.

Help small children learn that problems should not be feared. As they mature help them begin to learn the fundamentals of problem solving. Early successes stimulate self-confidence. Let them try to reach solutions on some problems all by themselves, knowing that they will make errors in this endeavor the way we all do in any new undertaking. Be there to help them try again. Encourage them. Errors aren't failures. Errors are merely guideposts that tell one what not to try the next time. It has been said that the wisest men are those who have made the most errors **and** have learned something useful from every single one of them.

Trouble-proofed kids are not problem-proofed kids; they are, however, problem identifying kids, problem analyzing kids, and problem-solving kids. Too often trouble-prone kids are problem avoiding kids who are far better at finding ways to escape from a problem than at even considering that it may, in fact, have a solution.

It is essential that parents be consistent in the way they approach their children and in the way they enforce the rules and expectations they set. To ease up on rule enforcement temporarily or as a special treat, only adds problems for the young child who has difficulty with the concept of temporary - thinking instead that any change will last forever only to be disappointed and confused when the lax time comes to an end.

One of the surest ways to create a trouble-prone kid is to only do to or for him, those things that you know will make him like you. The responsibility of the parent is, I believe, to do to or for the child those things that will help him grow into a self-confident, responsible, likeable, happy, socially beneficial, human being. During the process of preparing him there will be many times that what he needs to experience will not be what he wants to experience at that moment, and when we force the issue, we can fully expect to be less than popular with him for a while. But it is our responsibility to help the child know what we believe is right and wrong, and to help him or her grow toward independence and self-confidence. When we do this successfully the child will no longer need us, but, happily, he will still want us.

In general, the term discipline is a most misunderstood and therefore confusing concept. The dictionary tells us it is first, the ability to follow a set of rules and regulations, and second, that it is training that develops such self-control. Try to begin thinking about discipline as a positive, useful, state of mind that we want the child to achieve - an end result - rather than as a method of making him behave, such as punishment. When the training method is based on the belief in a socially beneficial set of values (such as the eight tenets), when it uses rewards for desired behaviors and ignores non-injurious types of undesired behavior, and when it emphasizes effective problem solving techniques, you are almost guaranteed a trouble-proofed child.

Finally, we talked about how to raise decisive, trouble-proofed kids, especially teenagers. I suggested that the formula was simple. Parents must help each of their children come to know exactly what he values and what he believes represents right and wrong behaviors. Then, in an instant, he can compare the present opportunity out in the world with those inner rules, and make a high quality, trouble-proofed, decision. If that opportunity fits those beliefs, he goes ahead. If it doesn't, he leaves the scene immediately or doesn't get involved.

We talked about setting our priorities in life in such a way as to assure that our families and our children are trouble-proofed forever. I suggested several ways to determine which of all your priorities are really and truly the most fundamentally important to you, so you can pursue a style of living that is in line with them, rather than the more superficial and less truly important aspects of life.

The next chapter concerns a topic vital to trouble-proofing and helping children grow into useful, productive, happy adults. It is included, here, to emphasize, that until we regain a true and lasting sense of the absolute preciousness of life, of human beings, and of concepts such as trust and helpfulness, it makes very little difference how we approach our children, because their world will soon come to a terrifying and permanent end.

/

Chapter Six:
A SENSE OF PRECIOUS

MANKIND'S MISSING INGREDIENT?

It is my purpose in this chapter to define what I believe is a crucial and distressing social and psychological problem, determine its probable extent, speak about its possible causes, and finally, suggest a specific course of treatment. My hope is that it will induce thoughtful consideration on your part and generate a sense of urgency that will impel you to action. Although I do believe there can be an extraordinary, bright light at the end of this frightening and somber tunnel, I am genuinely concerned that the tunnel, itself, may well collapse before we will be able to reach it.

What is a SENSE of PRECIOUS?

Some time ago, I had occasion to revisit my hometown and to review the headlines that had appeared in its newspaper just prior to World War II. "Craig Wins All-state Marathon Swim," "Bonnie Miller Takes Three Firsts At Fair," "Library Fund Goal Over The Top," "Retiring Teacher Feted - Hundreds Pay Tribute," "Chief Says Children's Safety Sole Issue In New Oak Street

Speed Limit." Weren't those refreshing headlines! Weren't they wonderfully people-centered? Weren't they reflective of the high esteem in which that little community held its precious citizens!

I became curious - a trait, which, as a child, I had acquired and homed in that same small community. For the sake of comparison, I contrasted those older headlines with some of that same paper's more recent banners: "Two Killed In Violent Weekend," "Break-in Discovered At Local Store," "Protesters Mar May Day Festivities," "Police Warn Citizens To Lock Doors," "Youth Charged In Assault On Elderly Couple." How sad and disquieting those tall, black lines of print had become during the forty years since that place had been my place, my sanctuary, and my home.

I had to wonder so many things. Just what was it that had changed? What was it that was now missing? What did we once have in that wonderful little community that is no longer there? How had that fine quality - whatever it was - escaped? What had forced it to leave?

I walked the streets and talked with the people. They were mostly strangers to me now but seemed to be nice people - perhaps a bit more reluctant than they used to be to strike up a conversation with an outsider. They seemed to still care about their little town - though I now heard many more complaints about its services. So, it was the same and it was different from when I was a barefoot boy, racing here and there, speaking to everyone in sight, with no one ever failing to wave or call back to me - each one reminding me to behave myself. I wondered: "Had these people changed the headlines, or had the headlines changed the people? Perhaps it was some combination of both? Perhaps neither?"

It is, of course, not just my little 'Springfield' that has changed. The Country as a whole and most of the World has changed in these same ways. Well, that's not really an accurate statement. It is not the Town, the Country, or the World - not the non-living things - that have changed. It is the people in that town, in this Country, in our World that have changed. But changed how? What elements or traits are gone? Which qualities, if any, have replaced them?

While sitting there on the old stone wall that surrounded the city park - one of my favorite thinking spots when I had been a teenager - an idea came to me. It was more of a question, I suppose: "Could it be that people just aren't as precious to one another as they once were? Could that in part, at least, explain the changes?" I sat a bit longer and wondered a bit more. From the vantage point of my nostalgic perch, I witnessed the good citizens of Springfield hurry by without so much as acknowledging my presence. Somehow, the warm memories of my yesterday just didn't fit the far cooler reality of that today.

Weeks later, in the unexpectedly more comfortable setting of my den, I pulled out my dictionary. It defined precious as that which is considered valuable or cherished. As synonyms for valuable, it further suggested words such as rare, exceptional, dear, and priceless. For cherished it provided the words loved, adored, and revered. That confirmed my understanding that precious refers to that which we each believe is one of the absolutely most significant and treasured aspects of our life. It is that which is most important to us – that, which we would protect at all cost. Precious! Those most valuable and cherished things that we can possibly imagine.

I suppose if we were each to list the half dozen things in our lives that fit that "preciousness" description for us, it would tell a great deal about us, wouldn't it. I was intrigued enough to make such a list for myself. How about you? ... What do you suppose your list would contain? Would there be stuff - such as wealth, a house, a car or jewelry? Would there be personal honors, status, or position, which you have achieved? Would there be comfort and affluence?   Would there be personal traits, such as appearance, strength, intelligence, compassion? Would there be goals for yourself, your family, and mankind? Would there be special relationships and people, such as your spouse, parents, children, friends - even all members of the human race, perhaps? Would it be your relationship with a supreme power? Would it be life, itself? There are so many possibilities, aren't there!

The thesis of this presentation is that if the human species is to survive in a form that confirms, practices, and enjoys its own remarkably unique characteristics, (which I believe are matchless in all of the known universe), it is human life and living that must be at, or very near, the top of every person's Precious List. Human life and living must come before stuff, and status, and comfort, and flattering or powerful personal traits. Human life and our right - if not obligation - to live it fully, safely, and cooperatively, must become unconditionally precious to all of us. I think it used to be that way for most people, especially for those living in the more rural regions of our society. I just don't see it as being that way today.

As a psychologist, educator, and social philosopher I have, for many years, worked to understand and assist individuals and families who are experiencing pain or turmoil in their lives, as well as those who regularly impose such pain and turmoil on others. It is my considered observation that there is no sense of the universal preciousness of human life and living among the pain inflictors of the World. Those would include the drive-by gunmen, the con artists, the conflict instigators, the thieves, the bullies, the hate-mongers, the spouse and child abusers, those who kill for kicks or for a few dollars, and those who, in other ways, shamelessly take advantage of their fellow human beings. However, where I have found that this crucial trait does exist, there have typically been no inhumane pain inflictors. When all human life and the process of living it rank near the top of our List of most precious things, then we live our lives in those ways that ensure that individuals, relationships, families, society, and mankind itself, all flourish and grow and become enriched.

What is the opposite of precious?

One might logically assume, I suppose, that the opposite of precious would be worthless, useless, or unwanted. In my experience, when applied to the realm of human relationships, more often than not the opposite of precious turns out to be, insignificant. It appears to me that people who have a well-defined sense of precious can be characterized as caring, empathetic, nurturing, and altruistic. On the other hand, those who see other human beings as insignificant, can be described as indifferent or self-serving - some, even pointlessly belligerent.

The person who is indifferent to other human beings assumes there is no reason to reach out and help those in need, or those who are hurting, or those who have lost their way, or those who have just not had the appropriate opportunities to acquire necessary skills or values. Those conditions are seen strictly as the problems of the folks who have them. It is the mentality so clearly reflected in the saying: "My responsibility ends at the tip of my nose."

It seems to me these folks fail to understand that living in need, in hardship, in despair, or in ignorance, breeds monumental personal and social problems that inevitably boil over and destroy the freedoms and comforts that the rest of us enjoy. When those-who-don't-have, decide to just take what they need or want, our safety, our comfort, our resources, and our freedoms are all diminished - the very existence of such privileges is threatened. As one simple example: When those parents who seemingly haven't a clue as to how to go about raising positive, loving, mentally healthy, productive, cooperative children, continue to unload their maladjusted offspring onto the World, the happiness and well-being of the rest of us is unquestionably at risk. Working to help improve those parents' child-rearing skills, would, therefore, actually be helping all of us.

A mankind that remains indifferent to the needs and requirements of others will surely destroy itself. Indifference can never be a legitimate choice - not for those of us who cherish the human species and its grand potential, or even for those who more selfishly desire to continue their own coveted version of the good life. If the basis of indifference is, as I have suggested, the belief that other human beings are insignificant, and if that belief is leading to the systematic destruction of mankind, and if insignificant is the destructive social opposite of precious, then it behooves us all - altruistic and selfish, alike - to actively cultivate, support, teach, and advocate the development of this sense of precious in all people, everywhere - especially in the children.

Where does it begin?

On numerous occasions, and in several pieces where I have written, I have referred to the following account, told to me by a very wise, very old, American Indian - Native American, if you prefer (he called himself and Indian). It is so insightful and so sound that it bears repeating. It relates to child rearing and the development of one's most basic personality traits.

"During the first three years of life a child watches how others treat him and listens to what they have to say about him. From these experiences he learns what kind of person they think he is. He then spends the remainder of his life attempting to prove them correct. If he has been treated with kindness and respect, has been praised, has had his important needs met, and has been joyfully and unconditionally accepted into the family, he learns that he is a good and treasured person. If his needs have been neglected and he has been treated roughly, and with contempt and ridicule, he learns that he is bad, a bother, a troublemaker, worthless, and he lives his life accordingly."

Aside from our present knowledge about some genetic predispositions and the effects on personality of some chemical imbalances and types of neurological damage, that old gentleman pretty well summarized, in a single paragraph, the essence of modern-day studies of personality development.

So, where does it begin? Where does the acquisition of this sense of the preciousness of all human beings get its start? In the home - early! It comes from the parents and all those who, early on, impact the child's beliefs about himself and others. Only when he learns that he, himself, is precious, can he begin to understand that all others are also precious. When he sees that he is expected to treat all others as though they are precious, then he begins to believe that might be true. When he is surrounded with people who he can readily experience as precious, then he knows it is true. When he realizes others still think he is precious even when he has made mistakes or has misbehaved, he begins to understand the unconditional nature of preciousness - that regardless of an individual's action at the moment, the value of that person and his life, remains precious.

How can this sense of precious be nurtured?

It all begins no later than the day one is born. (Some have argued convincingly that it begins even sooner, with the way the mother cares for herself during her pregnancy, thereby reducing certain physical stresses on the fetus.) I have detailed the importance of the earliest aspects of this process in my book, The Secrets of Deep Mind Mastery, and at this point, I will summarize and paraphrase a short portion of that presentation.

There is a necessary and essential set of infant care experiences that absolutely sets the stage for a happy, productive, trusting life. Of course, even after having had these necessary infant experiences, things may occur later on that prevent such a fine life, but the point is, without having had these experiences in the first place, a well-adjusted adult life, is just not possible – not, naturally, at least.

In simple terms, if you are raised one way as a baby, you have a great shot at a happy life in which you respect yourself and others, but if you're raised another way you are always going to be in for a rough, if not terrible time of it. In the second case the use of certain self-help programs or therapeutic techniques may be able to fix things up pretty well, provided the person is determined to improve his or her situation and finds competent guidance.

This set of necessary, infant, and early childhood experiences begins with a tender and always present kind of physical intimacy - physical contact. It includes being gently held, touched, patted, stroked, embraced, hugged, rocked, moved, and played with in ways that produce other pleasant physical sensations and experiences. (No intentionally painful or uncomfortable physical contacts.)

It includes being talked to in quiet, loving tones, and having the baby's own verbal sounds always responded to immediately and pleasantly by those around it - pleasant responses to the baby's crying as well as to its own more pleasant cooing and jabbering. (No yelling or ignoring.)

It includes adequate nourishment supplied when the baby needs it. (No periods of hunger or long delays in feeding.)

It includes timely bodily waste management, that is, clean and dry diapers and other clothing immediately when needed. (No long periods of being wet or messy.)

It includes adequate temperature control - cool enough when it is hot and warm enough when it is cold.

It includes a regular schedule for sleeping and being awake, for eating, playing, and bathing. (The lack of a dependable routine, makes the World totally unpredictable and therefore seem fearfully undependable, especially to an infant who has no language skills to assist him in trying to understand and control it.)

These several positive conditions lead immediately to the development of a Deep Mind that is based on a sense of safety and trust and self-worth. It helps the child learn, at a feeling-level, that its body and its physical needs are good things that he or she never has to be ashamed of. When the infant experiences a World that meets these needs - the only important needs that it understands, like food, cleanliness, temperature, tenderness, comfort, routine, social responses and attentiveness - it knows (senses) from the very beginning that this is a safe, helpful, trustworthy World it has entered. It senses that: "Since the people here are taking such good care of me, I must be a very precious, worthy little being."

Now these feelings and this knowledge about the World are not, of course, learned in so many words. All of this begins occurring way before language is meaningful. It is, nonetheless, stored as vivid and lasting impressions, deep, deep, down in the nonverbal, feelings compartment of the Deep Mind. These earliest experiences form the child's very first and most influential entries into his or her Deep Mind. From then on they become the automatic basis for directing the person's reactions, his expectations about himself, and the nature of the World. They answer the two questions that are always at the forefront of the Deep Mind, "At this moment, is this probably a safe or a harmful World?" and, "What is my role supposed to be in this World right now?"

To the degree that this sequence of positive experiences is not met, poor adjustment, fears, uncertainties, non-dependability, self-doubt, unhappiness, and other hurtful characteristics and expectations begin to grow and interfere with personal adjustment and interpersonal relationships. If, early on, life seems to be cold, hurtful, and filled with uncertainties, then those are the things the person comes to expect from the World. And what kind of person would other people treat in that way? One who they believed was precious, or one to whom they were indifferent? On the other hand, if life is warm, comforting, and dependable, then that is the way the infant expects the World to be. And what kind of person would other people treat in those ways? One who they believed was precious or one to whom they were indifferent?

Part of you may be saying, "But, sometimes, or even often, the World is all of those bad things. Why should I prepare an infant to expect a good World when he or she is soon going to discover that it sucks?" My friend, your World, the one you experience every day, just doesn't have to suck. I don't care how bad it may seem on the surface. It's virtually all in the way you define that World, but that is another topic, and it is explained and developed in the previously mentioned book, Deep Mind Mastery.

So, a sense of precious is instilled early on by a specific set of positive, infant care, procedures. Then, later, as the child grows and matures, these very same attributes must continue to be fostered. Even as behavior correction becomes necessary (once the child is old enough to know the difference between right and wrong), it, too, must be carried out in ways that help the child understand that he or she is still precious. It is only the behavior or underlying value that is unacceptable.

As time goes on, additional approaches need to be utilized. Praise rather than condemnation is the approach of choice. Encouragement rather than ridicule or belittling. Inclusion rather than exclusion. Freedom, as is age-appropriate and value-appropriate, rather than restraint. These will lead to other necessary and positive traits such as determination rather than indecision, willingness to try new things (within the bounds of safety and good judgment) rather than reluctance, feelings of proficiency rather than inferiority, and gratefully accepting mistakes and failures as helpful guideposts that tell one what to avoid the next time.

Taken as a whole, these positive approaches to a child's upbringing, when used consistently, through the years, will prove to him that he is thoroughly and unconditionally precious.

The next essential step in our process can then develop and emerge - to make the rational connection that if I can assume that this one human being (me) is precious, then I must assume that other human beings are precious, also. When the child has achieved this step, he will forever be one of the good guys - one of the good and helpful human beings. In some ways, life then becomes easier, because he never has to do things just to prove his own worth or importance, or to extract reassuring, worth establishing, complements from others. When he does nice and helpful things for others it is solely because he wants to and not in order to glean some positive recognition for his good deed.

When he is unable to achieve this step, he will, most likely, become one of the pain inflictors - one of the indifferent - one of those who will propel mankind toward its own destruction, or in the least, do nothing to prevent it. As if that is not bad enough, he will probably do so without even recognizing what he is doing. As the saying goes, self-centered, self-serving, people seldom do see beyond the ends of their noses. The long-term effects of their thoughtless and greedy lifestyle escape them completely. They have acquired, you see, that terrifying, and always devastating sense of indifference. To them, the rest of us have become the insignificant. Often, nothing, including themselves, is more than fleetingly precious. All things only have meaning for the moment. Life itself has become relatively valueless. These people have denied, or at least overlooked, those remarkable human characteristics, which allow us to live a uniquely caring and wonder-filled life - one not available to any other known life form in the universe. They have misplaced the sense of precious. In discovering this, though, perhaps we have found mankind's missing ingredient. Hopefully we can find ways to restore it in time - in time to save our children; in time to save our World; in time to save our species.

I have a story I really want to relate here, but I am reluctant to do so because it may seem to have a boastful tone to it. I suppose, however, since it presents my message in, what I think is a wonderfully poignant nutshell, I'll bow to my sense of urgency and assume you will pardon a parent's pride.

When my son was about ten and a half, he asked to be filled in about the birds and bees - "And don't leave anything out!" were the final, duly emphasized words in his request. Aside from commenting that he thought certain parts of the explanation were, in his words, "absolutely revolting," he also went on to a more thoughtful note, "So, I'm alive because of you and Mom!" he pondered, quietly. The conversation ended.

On the morning of his eleventh birthday, his mother and I found, on the breakfast table, two small packages, wrapped with all the care an eleven-year-old boy could possibly muster. Each contained a ring - mine with a blue stone - my favorite color - his mother's, with a pink stone - her favorite color. Beside them on the table, there was this simple, hand scrawled note: "Dear Mom and Dad: Thank you for giving me life. Your son, Franklin."

And on each of his birthdays thereafter, we, again, received little gifts along with that same, simple, wonderful note.

It appears to me, that his Mother and I had done something right in this "precious" department.

How can we go about restoring this sense of precious?

Let's roll up our sleeves and get practical, down to earth, and absolutely realistic about how we do this. How do we restore this sense of precious to the nature of mankind? We do it one person at a time, of course. It will be easier if we are attempting to do it with the very young children who are in our care, rather than with the adolescent or the adult who is already well down the path toward indifference.

Still, let's see what specific suggestions we can make here and now. Remember, it is my position that this well-developed sense of precious, will prevent such things as breaking the law, vandalism, stealing, bloodshed, beatings, killings, looting, rioting, scamming, cheating, conning, illicit drug use, and the biggest threat of all, war itself.

Think about this for a moment. Would a person, who

believed that all human life was precious, ever be moved to maliciously kill someone? Would someone who truly saw the laws of the land as precious, be moved to riot, loot, or even speed or litter? Would someone who believed without a doubt that trust was a precious characteristic, ever routinely engage in lying, cheating, scamming, libeling or slandering others? In 99% of all situations, the answers to these questions would have to be NO, a person with a well-defined sense of precious would just not engage in those kinds of activities.

Without rules, social groups just cannot function, can they? Think about the smallest of the social groups, the family. Families just have to have at least some rules, don't they? Without rules or expectations about what each member is or is not to do, and when and how those responsibilities are to be carried out, there would be utter and absolute chaos.

The same goes, of course, for larger social groups like towns, cities, states, countries and the international community. Rules, or laws as we call them when a government establishes them, are the means by which we are able to maintain control, personal safety, peace, cooperation, healthful conditions, and in general, assure our over-all wellbeing. When rules or laws are merely seen as guidelines that can either be broken or adhered to, according to whatever pleases an individual at the moment, then the whole concept of law and order vanishes. We have undeniable proof of that all around us, don't we? Either we all learn to faithfully abide by all of the rules, or our wellbeing is, diminished and threatened.

Let's examine one of the examples, mentioned above. It is always the least popular of those examples, when I am talking with groups of people - speeding. Tell me, could you think of good ways to spend twelve billion dollars? Could you find things that much money might be used for that would truly benefit mankind, and very likely yourself, in the process? - New roads, improved medical care, increased social security benefits, improved schools, tremendously reduced taxes, early childhood education? That is the amount of money it is estimated we could save if we didn't have to patrol our highways, looking for speeders and didn't have to pay for the damages and pain, speeders inflict each year.

Why do we have speed limits? Is it just to make life miserable for those who are in a hurry? Of course not! Trite as it may sound, "Speed kills." It is just that plain and simple. There is no way of intelligently arguing with the data on that subject. If speeders only maimed and killed themselves, it might be a shade different, but they don't just maim and kill themselves, do they? So, if we each obeyed all speed limits, all of the time, we would need no speed cops, would we? However, so long as people only obey a law because they think they may be punished if caught disobeying it and not because they agree the laws themselves are good, - that is precious - then we will just have to go on wasting all of that money used to hire policeman to be on the lookout for those who break that one law.

Well, back to the more central point here. Developing a sense in all of us, from our very earliest days, that all of our rules and laws are precious, is absolutely essential. When there are laws, we feel are bad laws, we have legal processes that really do work to repeal or change them. That is one of the wonderful things about the democratic process. It may not be easy. It may be time consuming, but it can almost always be accomplished. I am not arguing here for or against the concept of civil disobedience when all legal courses for improving some terrible ongoing human injustice have been tried and failed. I am speaking about that 95% of all rules and laws that do make good sense and are for the basic and real benefit of us all.

The bottom line here is simply that we need to help our youngsters understand that the rules we have - assuming they are well thought through, are reasonable, and are appropriate for the age level and skill level of the child - are to be followed without fail. It must be consistently obvious that they are not to just be followed when the child feels like it, or when the parent feels up to enforcing them, but that they are to be followed all of the time.

Over the years, my wife and I enjoyed having many foster children in our home. During their first week with us, most of them were flabbergasted that, once the rules had been made clear to them, we didn't give second chances, or warnings when it came to following those rules. When I'd hear protests like, "But that's not fair. Everybody deserves a second chance," my response was, "I wouldn't have the rule if it weren't important in the first place, and in the first place doesn't mean in the second place."

A rule is a rule and requiring that children follow it every single time is the only way to help youngsters learn that rule following is an essential part of living in a society. The big World provides no second chances when it comes to ignoring many of its rules. So, when a child grows up thinking that he can always disregard a rule at least once before it will actually be enforced, he is in for major trouble down the road. The more relevant point, here, is that when the child knows that we believe he is totally capable of following the rules, he learns something very special about himself - about our confidence in his ability, about one more precious attribute he possesses as an intelligent, caring, human being.

The child must see that the important models in his life - Mom, Dad, siblings, etc. - also all follow all of the rules and laws all of the time. Otherwise, raising an honest, rule-following youngster doesn't have a chance of happening. When rules are seen as the child's friends, as guidelines that benefit him and others in the long run - in the big picture - then rules and laws can become precious. When they are precious, they will be obeyed, protected, and modeled for those even younger eyes that are always around, watching and learning.

The impact of our throw-away society

We will now move on to another area that seems important as we examine this topic of precious. In our present day, throwaway, society it is sometimes difficult to help our children develop a sense of precious when it comes to possessions. When something breaks or gets lost, or needs painting or mending, we toss it out and get a new one. If I may interject here just one of those always groan-producing tales from the olden days, I promise I won't do so again. (Well, promise may be to strong a word!)

Anyway, when I was a little boy - as these stories always begin - things were just not replaced so readily. If a doll or a toy truck broke, or if my trousers got a rip in the knee from a fall on the sidewalk, we learned how to fix them. If the wagon lost its finish, we sanded it down and repainted it. If the toaster stopped heating, grandpa took it apart and made it as good as new again. We kept things. We were proud of our things. Our things became very precious to us. We would never have wanted to give up our treasured possessions and have to go out and replace them with something new. A new substitute was never as desirable as the original.

You may have heard the story about the old carpenter who was so proud of his hammer - one his father had given to him years before. Now, he had replaced the head twice and the handle four times, but it was the same old hammer as far as that old man was concerned, and it was precious.

I remember as a four-year-old I had a doll, a truck, a ball, and a special little box that locked. That was about the extent of my toys. I built other things of course out of match boxes and folded newspaper, and scraps of this and that, but in terms of real toys, I had very few. And, having very few, each one became very precious. Looking into the typically overflowing toy chest of a four-year-old today, I find it not at all surprising that the youngster has no conception of precious, when it comes to possessions.

When children have long-term possessions, that become precious to them, they can begin to understand how precious the possessions of others are to them. This makes them think at least twice before damaging or borrowing or taking another's toy or bike or car. The child can well imagine, deep down inside, how it would feel to lose something precious. If we have successfully helped the child learn that all those other people out there are truly precious, he will tune into their feelings about their things, and will refrain from violating their property.

So, we help our children develop a sense of the preciousness of things. We help them learn about taking good care of their things. We help them learn that when they are careless with one of their possessions, the consequence is not that we just go get a new one, but, rather, that he lives with what has happened to it. Precious things are cared for, protected, kept track of and put safely away after use. Insignificant things are _____, well, I'm sure you can fill in that blank.

Making people precious

How do children learn that other people are precious? I have generalized about it earlier, but let's look at some specific techniques. You know, at this point I'm really glad I didn't make that a full-fledged promise earlier, because I feel another old-time story about to burst loose. My family had several rules about life that have served me well through the years, so, for whatever they may be worth to you, I want to present them here.

It is useful, I think, for you to first know that we were poor. (My father was a teacher back the day when teachers were among the very poorest paid folks in the land.) Until my High School graduation, I had seldom had dress-up clothing bought in a store - Mom made it for me or friends or relatives handed it down to me. I don't remember ever having had a brand-new store-bought toy as a young child. Well, again, you get the picture. I hasten to add that it was *only* in terms of money and new things that we were poor. In all other ways, we had a rich and wonderful life together.

Back to the story. Two of the rules of living, which were followed by my parents, are of interest in the context of this topic. The first was that ten percent of all our income was given away to assist those who were less fortunate than we were. When I earned a dime, mowing a lawn, I knew that a penny went into the "Help Jar" on the kitchen cabinet. When Mom earned a dollar for doing a washing ten cents was added immediately to that jar. About once a month, we counted the money and decided how it would be used - who it would be used to help. It was, I remember, a time of great joy for all of us, and some of our discussions became quite animated as we gradually narrowed the field and finally agreed on a project, we all felt was worthy.

Whenever possible, that project, as Mom referred to the undertaking, was done anonymously. Dad said that when you took credit for a good deed, it made it less special. It wasn't the credit that was the point - it was only the deed that mattered. Do you suppose that I learned, early in life, that other people were pretty precious things? Once you have the opportunity to genuinely help others, you can't help but learn something about how precious they are.

We also had another jar into which another ten percent of all earnings went. It was marked, "Rainy Day," and we all knew it would be there whenever we really needed it. This helped me realize that my welfare was also precious, but that was not the second rule of life I wanted to relate to you.

Every Sunday afternoon, after we had eaten our extra-delicious, noon-time dinner, and had made some special plans for the coming week, we set out together to do something helpful for someone outside of our family. Sometimes we just visited an old couple or someone who was ill. Often, we did yard work for those who couldn't do it for themselves. Dad was quite a carpenter, and with my help, we sometimes repaired fences, porches or banging window shutters. In season, we helped garden, mow lawns and shovel snow. Mom would often help with the house cleaning or canning while Dad and I did the outside things. When we were finished, we never failed to tell each other what a good day it had been. And it always had been just that. Again, I learned not only how precious those others were who had needed my help, but how precious I was, because I had skills I could use to make their lives better, and because I had the genuine desire to be helpful.

People were truly important to each other back then. We depended on one another, not only for help, but also for our entertainment - conversation, table games, word games, ball games - you name it. When you depended on others in those ways, they became a very precious part of your life. Can families still do these kinds of things today? I see no reason why they can't. Perhaps ten percent for charity may seem too steep (of course Dad said if it wasn't a sacrifice, it wasn't actually charity), but how about even two percent or five percent? Children learn that other people are precious when they see the adults around them treating all people as though they are precious. There is no secret to it. It's just that simple.

Why has being helpful to others become such a lost art in so many homes? We can blame the TV or movies or what have you, but the fact is, TV's are built with an "Off" button, and Movies aren't vital to one's survival. Some can say the neighborhood is too unsafe to venture into to, but what about the person across the hall or street, or how about making and sending cards to people whose lives you know would be brightened by receiving them. Even a four-year-old can help draw the pictures. How about phone calls to shut-ins or to those who you know are lonely. Kids love to talk on the phone. Be creative! That is one of the human being's greatest and most unique qualities!

I know an older woman in a poor section of a large city who keeps an assortment of beautiful, blooming plants in her front window for all to see as they pass by. They are clearly arranged to be seen by those looking in from outside. All the neighbors appreciate that tiny little bright spot in the otherwise blighted area in which they live. Without leaving her apartment, Mrs. Gretzki has found a way to help her fellow man, and to let them know their welfare is important to her.

Perhaps, being helpful has become a lost art simply because we now have a generation for which other people are no longer precious. How sad this is, if true. How devastating. How final, for mankind. But how wonderful it is that one of the human beings' finest strengths, is that it can change, grow and mature. It can recognize the inadequacy of its past behaviors and do something about it, almost immediately. It can be positive and energetic and filled with purpose; it can look to the future, and modify its own course of action, in order to save its own future generations - something no other life form in all of the known universe can do.

Pride and an appreciation for new knowledge

What are some other things we can do in our quest to put this sense of precious back into the automatic nature of mankind? When children learn to take pride in what they do, they gain a sense of how precious a job well done can be, as well as how precious they are for being able to do it. The human species can never hope to become all that it is capable of becoming until we each strive to individually make ourselves into that most wonderful being that we can possibly become. This doesn't happen when we are willing to settle for a, "just getting by," level of workmanship. This doesn't happen when we settle for going to work, coming home to the TV and then going to bed, only to mindlessly repeat this stifling and self-centered routine day after day.

Every week, I hear young workers say things to the effect that if their supervisor didn't complain, then they felt they had done a good enough job. I hear no sense of pride. There is no implication that they have tried to do the best they can do. There is no recognition of how precious their individual skills or contributions are. Quite simply, just getting by, has replaced pride in a job well done. This is thoroughly frightening to me!

I hear the same about their schoolwork. "I passed, and that's all that is important," is so frequently the message. I almost never hear, "I learned something really fantastic today," or "Tomorrow we get to begin a chapter about such and such and I'm really excited that I'm going to finally get to find out about that." Knowledge just doesn't seem to be a precious commodity anymore.

Of course, some of today's young people are excited about learning. Some young people do strive to do well at their jobs and with their other responsibilities. But it no longer seems to be nearly such a universal trait as I believe it used to be - OR that it has to be. How can we make learning and doing well, again acquire a precious priority in the lives of all of our youngsters?

Of course, seeing these traits in the adult models who surround them, is the most efficient and effective way to influence the acquisition of these or any qualities. Parents who read to their children, early on, let them know how precious books and knowledge are. Parents who take the time to patiently answer children's questions, let them know how precious wanting to learn is. Parents who, from day one, expect the child to do as well as he can do - no more, no less - instill a sense of the preciousness of self-acceptance and self-esteem, that results from a job well done. Parents who present a positive example and encourage their children to, "Do as I do," and never resort to the tired and always self-tarnishing, "Do as I say, not as I do," have a genuine chance of restoring a sense of precious to our youngest, most recent, edition of mankind.

On the other hand, parents who are unwilling or unable to be such positive, helpful, models, present major problems for the future of mankind. When a child looks at one or both of his parents, and realizes that that parent possesses little, if anything, to recommend him as being precious, what does that make the child think about himself as the one who was born of that parent? As one disturbing example of such a condition, what do fatherless children learn about the responsibility taking skills of adult males? And, if that child is a boy, what does all this suggest to him about himself, his personal potential, and his own anticipated role in life a few years down the road?

The final choice?

Sometime ago, I had several teenagers read an early draft of the material that I have presented here. We then got together on several occasions so they could give me their impressions, ask questions and make suggestions. One was a fifteen-year-old boy who found himself in a detention home for the sixth time in three years. One was an honor student in a local high school. One was a dishwasher, after school and evenings, saving for a car. One was the daughter of a college professor. One was an average student, the son of a single, working mother.

Their unanimous impression was that this had been at once the most frightening and the most hope-filled piece they had ever read. It was frightening in that they all saw the necessity for a sense of precious, yet only one of them felt he really had it. It was frightening, in that the World they knew, was, indeed a World, generally without a sense of precious, either among their fellow adolescents or in the adults they knew. It was frightening, in that although they saw the necessity for possessing this sense of precious, they really didn't want to give up the admittedly self-indulgent, self-centered, selfish lifestyle they had assumed and liked.

It was hope-filled to them, in that it presented an answer to a question they had all contemplated at one time or another during that past year: "What's missing in my life and the lives of my friends?" As one of them put it somewhat cryptically, "Even when we're happy we're not happy." It was hope-filled in that, even though four of them were not optimistic about finding this sense of precious themselves, they thought if others would just obtain it, the World might have some chance of surviving. In the end, it was hope-filled, in that they thought if their memory of our discussions troubled them enough, perhaps, someday they would try to do something about it, after all. One of the girls suggested she certainly wanted the daycare people who would eventually be tending her children, to be good models, "in this whole preciousness thing."

At one point, the sole holder of the precious trait broke into tears, pleading that the others do something to help. None of the others could understand what their young colleague was feeling at that point, nor why he would be crying about it. They had, from my perspective, little if any capacity for empathy.

To me, the experience was also both frightening and hope filled. It was frightening to me, in that these precious young people had so little hope for themselves or for the survival of the human species. It was frightening to me in that they had no motivation to change, even with their obviously accurate understanding of the critical magnitude of the problem. It was frightening to me, in that even that one member of their peer group, was totally unable to communicate his well-founded sense of urgency to them.

It was hope-filled to me, in that at least one out of five understood about precious, and treasured the fact that his upbringing had provided it for him. It was hope-filled to me in that they had all been genuinely troubled by the problem, and at least recognized that it existed, full-blown, on every street and in every block. It was hope-filled to me in that they were willing to come back on four separate occasions, of their own volition, and talk together and with me for two and three hours at a stretch, as we probed this important topic together. It was hope-filled to me in that, although during all of this time they had not seen themselves acquiring a sense of precious, I had. As limited a change as it may have been, they would never again feel as indifferent as they had before. Other human beings would never again be quite as insignificant as they had seemed before. Without realizing it, they were far more open and ready to change than they had ever suspected, and that was and is hope-filled!

So, what is our final choice? <u>Without</u> a deeply instilled and regularly practiced sense of precious, and thereby forsaking our remarkable and unique human qualities and potentials, mankind is, I believe, headed down the road to continued self-inflicted misery, and toward an existence not unlike that of the so-called lower animals. <u>With</u> this all-important sense of precious, however, I believe that not only are we not doomed to a subhuman existence, but that mankind's finest and most enlightened and fulfilling days still stretch out before us.

It is my fondest hope and dream that those of you who share my concern about this issue, will become ardent and fervent purveyors of this sense of precious in all that you do and with all those you meet. Reinforce it where you see it happening. Encourage it where you feel it beginning to unfold. Teach it from scratch where it seems to be nonexistent. And, most important of all, model it in all that you do and say. If indeed, this sense of precious is the missing ingredient, and if its absence is responsible for some or most of mankind's current adversities, then we each have an urgent mission - return the sense of precious to the nature of mankind.

Let me conclude these thoughts with a very short, very true, very precious story. As I was sitting on a park bench not long ago, I was enjoying the simply beautiful day and was captivated by the children at play. Presently, I was approached by two five-year-old girls.

What's your name?" one of them asked.

"Kids usually just call me Grampa," I replied. "Can I know your names?"

The more forward of the two immediately said, "I'm Mary."

The other, mimicking my inflection, then added, "Mama usually calls me Precious."

I asked Precious what she thought that pretty name, meant.

Bright eyed and beaming, she replied, "Oh, it means I'm worth more than all the gold and diamonds in the whole World."

Mary gasped and put her hand to her mouth, looking absolutely astonished as she reported; "Well what do you know! That's exactly the same thing that *Mary* means!"

Two little girls, with two different Mamas, who had each done an exceptional job of helping their little ones come to understand what a true and priceless treasure we each have the grand privilege of experiencing, in this fleeting form we call a human being.

* * *

The final chapter is one that was prepared especially for the thirteen to eighteen-year-olds among us. It has as its goal the reinforcing of those important trouble-proofing approaches presented in the foregoing chapters. The adolescents, who take time to master its contents and apply them in their daily lives, will find that they have effectively trouble-proofed themselves.

/

Chapter Seven
A chapter especially for teens

It was nearly ten o'clock, on a cold, rainy, autumn evening when I answered the unexpected knock at my front door. I found myself face to face with a dripping wet young man in his late teens. I didn't recognize him and yet somehow, I knew him.

"Come in out of the weather," I said, all quite automatically, motioning him inside and closing the door behind him. "What can I do for you?"

He brushed back his dripping wet, long blond hair, tugged his drenched shirt away from his chest and smiled broadly as he answered. "You already done it, Doc."

As his story unfolded, I learned that more than two years before, he and I had talked - well, sort of talked - His probation officer had dragged him, kicking and screaming, to see me. Then I remembered - it had been a very short meeting because the lad refused to talk, except for occasional outbursts, during which he had strung together four-letter words in creative combinations that I'd never ever before heard.

I got the young man a towel and invited him to sit down as

he continued to speak.

"You saved my life, you know!" he said.

"How's that!" I asked, rapidly searching my memory to find what wonderful piece of advice I must have given him.

"You asked me what kind of a life I wanted to have built for myself by the time I reached age thirty."

I waited silently for more, but as it turned out, that was it."

He explained further: "I'd never thought about being thirty before, because I figured I'd be dead before I was even twenty. It started me thinking about how it would be to really grow up and really grow old. I liked the idea, you know. And when I asked myself how I could do that - get to grow old - the answer was right there in your question - I'd have to build my life, myself. I'd always just floated along like an empty beer can in a sewer - going wherever some new flush somewhere took me. But I suddenly realized I was more than a beer can. I was a person, and I could think, and I could plan, and I could decide how I wanted my life to grow. I could work to be somebody."

Suddenly it was five o'clock in the morning. We had talked the night away - well, mostly, he had, this time. It had been a wonderful night. I'm still not sure he realizes that it was really all his doing and not mine that helped him go back and finish high school, and get and keep an evening job, enroll in welding school, and make things right between him and his Mom. The point is, having a goal for the future and a plan to get you there, gives wonderful purpose to your life and helps us each find the strength and the courage to turn our lives around.

The point of this chapter, my friend, is to show you how it truly is possible to stay out of trouble forever and to build for yourself, a grand and exciting long life.

If, at this point, you decide to keep reading, and I hope you will, you are going to want to know some things about me. You're probably already asking yourself, "So, why does this old guy think he knows anything that could possibly help me?" That's an intelligent and important question. Let me try to answer it for you.

My name is Tom Gnagey (forget the first 'G'). Through the

years, I've had many great goals to work toward - some of them I've reached and some I haven't. They were all fun to try for! As a result, I did reach age thirty, myself, nearly fifty years ago. I'm still going strong - not bad for a poor kid who was convinced that he was a total freak during most of those years when he was growing up, and who worked very hard at trying to kill himself during the summer he was sixteen.

Let's see. How can I quickly help you get to know me? Maybe this will do it. You know, as we live our lives, we all wear a lot of different hats - we all have a lot of different roles to play, don't we. Let me list some of the roles I've played during my lifetime. I'm sure that many of them will be just like yours. Some will be different, of course. That's what makes it my own special life, different from yours and still a lot like yours. As you read about these various hats that I've worn, try to form a picture of who I have been and who I am today. Not even right now, of course, do I know what I'll decide to be in the future. That's part of the wonder-filled adventure of being a human being.

As you'll soon see, during my lifetime I've had the chance to be many different things. I've been a son, a cute little kid, an average looking bigger child, an adolescent with a dreadful complexion problem, a suicidal teenager, an adult, more recently an old-ish sort of person, a student, a boyfriend, an ex-boyfriend (having gotten dumped on more than a few occasions!), a competitive swimmer, a musician and composer, a sculptor, a carpenter, a husband, a father, a foster father, a widower, a best friend, a worst enemy, a grade school teacher, a high school teacher, a college professor, a counselor at orphanages and detention homes, a clinical psychologist, a poor person, a rich person, a homeless person, a worker in a dairy queen, kitchen help in a restaurant, and a writer of books for children, teens, parents, and senior citizens. Presently, I am attempting to become your friend and to help you in your search for ways to be a successful person, to love yourself and others, and to live a very, very happy and rewarding and trouble-free life, now, and in your future.

As I said, I'm quite sure that you have already been many of these same things, haven't you? We have both shared many of these same kinds of experiences. Since I am older, I experienced them first, and I experienced them in a different era, so I probably experienced them a little differently than you. But, basically, we have both been there, haven't we? We've both grown up knowing the great times and the sad times, the successes and failures. From time to time, we have both, felt confident, fearful, strong, and weak. We've even felt loved and unloved - wanted and not wanted. Some days and places we've fit in and some days and places we haven't.

Sometimes the teenage years seem impossible, don't they? Well, if nothing else, I am living proof that adolescence CAN be survived! Many grown-ups seem to want to just forget how it was to have been an adolescent. I never want to forget those years, because during them, I learned so much about life, about myself, and about other people - things that are still important to me to this very day. It's a tough time - adolescence - but it can also be an outstanding time - especially for those who are able to keep themselves out of trouble.

One of the continuing joys in my life is making new teenage friends. I am deeply interested in understanding what goes on in your minds. I enjoy listening to you and learning from you just how it is - today - being a part of your very special age group.

A little later in this chapter, I will introduce you to one of my all-time best, teenage friends, a remarkable seventeen-year-old young man named Jay, who decided to take control of himself, in order to turn his life around. A few short months before we met, his life was blindly plunging along toward certain self-destruction. Since then, Jay has begun building for himself a new, productive, self-disciplined life, and is now working toward creating what can certainly become a very bright and rewarding future.

Why am I so fond of Jay? For many of the same reasons that you will be, once you meet him. Partly, because he pulls no punches. If something doesn't make sense to him, or if he doesn't understand it, he's honest and just says so. He asks questions and keeps probing until he has found the answer he needs. He isn't afraid to admit when he doesn't know it all, and he always asks me the truly hard questions about life. I suppose that Jay reminds me a lot of myself at his age - a bit confused yet a bit wise, a bit frightened yet a bit brave, a bit child and yet a bit old man. I admire him for how steadily he keeps working at building himself into the kind of human being both he and I, and most others can respect. His goal is to become one of the good guys in the World. One who believes it is only right to be trustworthy and honest and who takes time to be kind and helpful to those around him - one who understands that, like it or not, he is a role model for those younger and less assured than he. Jay also appeals to me because he loves to have a good time and because he has a quick sense of humor, a most engaging laugh, bright flashing eyes, and a broad, easy smile, that immediately puts those around him at ease. And, as in any friendship, there are, of course, other more personal, reasons.

Before you meet Jay, however, I need to set the stage. First, I want to take you on a short trip back in time to an era in which life, for all of its regular, every day, kinds of problems, was a very good time in which to grow up. I know. The last thing you want to hear is some old codger spinning tales about the good old days. Well, what if we titled this story something like: "The town in which everyone could be trusted." Or what about, "The day principal Grungy got his shorts run up the flagpole?" Or let's try one more: "July 4th, 1944: The evening all the boys from Miss Prigg's eighth grade class, gathered on her front lawn and mooned her!"

Well, some things, you see, really don't change. But, some things have changed in very scary ways, and, in all honesty, that is the real point of this story. So, perhaps a more honest title would be, "Discovering the magic potion that will allow you and your children to live happily ever after." By whatever name, here's the story.

The town in which I grew up was a small town. There were fewer than a thousand people living there. Probably about two hundred of them were past sixty. Another three hundred were parents, which left about four hundred kids. That would average out to be about fifteen or twenty kids at each age level. In a town that size, everybody knew everybody else.

With so few kids at any age, we each soon learned it was important to keep them all as our friends. That was really, how it was, too. We all cared about each other. We helped each other out when someone needed us, and we knew, without any doubt, that we could count on the others should we ever need their help. Oh, we had our disagreements, don't get me wrong, but through it all, we cared about one another. (I got my first shiner at nine – it was what we called a doozie, back then.)

I lived with Mom and Pop, right at the city limits in a small white house with a board fence around it, a garden and fruit trees behind it, and a stream, complete with swimming hole just down the hill, in back. I'm quite certain that, right away, you would have noticed something strange about our front door. It didn't have a keyhole. There was no place for a key - no lock whatsoever. Neither did the back door, nor did hardly any other door in the whole town, except the bank. There was just no need for locks. None of us would have ever considered entering someone else's house without their permission.

One year, Pop needed a short-term loan. I remember watching as the banker counted out the money into Pop's hand. He and Pop agreed when it would be paid back, and they shook hands. There was no loan paper signed. There was no notarized agreement. A man's word and his handshake were all that were required, because we were honest people back then, in that little town where I grew up.

I remember one Sunday afternoon at an all town picnic in the park, Mrs. Wilkins lost her wedding ring. We all stopped what we were doing, and searched the park till dark and then, met again at dawn, Monday morning, to continue looking. Eventually my friend John found the ring in the grass. The whole town cheered and John, holding the ring high for all to see, was hoisted up onto the shoulders of several men as we all marched around, celebrating the find. Why would we all spend that much time looking for a fifty-dollar, ring? And why would we all be so overjoyed when it was found? It was because we all cared about Mrs. Wilkins. We all knew how precious that ring was to her, especially since her husband had recently been killed in the war. Also, our helping her was nothing less than she would have done for one any of us.

In my little town, none of us would have ever considered just passing someone on the sidewalk without speaking or stopping to ask about the family or complimenting them on their hat or shirt or the homer hit in the game the night before. We would always try to think of something to say that would brighten that other person's day. Why? Because we cared about them and we wanted their lives to be as fine as they could possibly be that day. And of course, they wished the same for us.

As I mentioned, I was one of the poor kids in my town, which meant that I didn't get to buy very many new things. Instead, when I wanted a new bike, I went to the city dump, found the parts I needed and built myself a bike. When I wanted bunk beds, I collected scrap lumber from the building sites in town and constructed a set. When I wanted a new room, I remodeled our attic with bits and pieces from all over the county. Was I sad that I couldn't afford to purchase brand new things? Never, so far as I can remember. In fact, I once wrote in my diary, how sorry I felt for the 'poor rich kids'. When they wanted something new, they had to just go out and buy it, thereby missing out on all of the joy and the feelings of pride and accomplishment that came with the planning and anticipation, and the process of building it themselves. If I needed some wood, I'd work out a deal with the lumberyard. I would shovel their walks in winter or wash their windows in the fall. If I needed a rug for my room or a new bedspread, I'd find some other skill that I could trade to a storekeeper. I didn't expect to receive anything free, in fact, I was raised to believe that was quite wrong. If you were a healthy, good, and honest person, you paid your own way. Anything less was dishonorable.

On July fifth, of the summer when I was sixteen, I slipped into a deep coma for several days. I was teetering on the brink of death during most of that time. Later, I was told that during it all, almost every kid in town, had gathered on the lawn outside Doc Smith's office, where he was caring for me. They just sat on the grass and talked or quietly sang reassuring songs that we all had known forever. The adults, when work and other responsibilities allowed, would stop by and sit with them for as long as they could spare.   The women of our church brought sandwiches and lemonade and Pastor would offer up a prayer now and then.

One of the first things I remember hearing after awakening on that hot July 9th morning, was a cheer to beat all cheers, as that crowd of my friends and neighbors received the news from Doc, that I was awake and was going to be ok. It wasn't that I was anyone more special than anyone else - in fact, you will remember, I was just an ordinary kid living as part of a poor family on the edge of town. The point is that that same thing would have happened for anyone. Why? Because we all truly cared about - loved if you will - each and every person there in our little community. We felt responsible for one another. When one of us was in pain, we were all in pain. When one of us was successful, we also all shared that grand happiness.

But you may be thinking, that just isn't how it is anymore, old man. Get real! It's different. Today, many people take advantage of each other - they cheat, lie, steal, vandalize, and use force and even kill to get what they want. I know all of that is true, but I also know that the capacity of people to be kind and gentle and caring has not just somehow vanished from the human species. I know that spark of concern for other's welfare still lives on deep down inside almost every one of us. It just needs the right environment to blossom again, and it is your generation, my young friend, that has the power to make this wonderful change occur. If it doesn't, the human species will soon go the way of the dinosaurs.

The older generation (the generation of your parents) has, for some reason that not even they, can explain, tried to live in a new way. It has been, I believe, an overly competitive, selfish, think only of myself and to hell with anyone else kind of way - and look where it has gotten them - well, even more sadly, look where it has gotten you. Young boys are killing each other every single day of the year. Old people are virtual prisoners of fear in their own homes. Many fathers remain so selfish and so immature that they won't take the responsibility to stay in the home and help care for their own children. Three generations of families, now, seem to prefer to be on welfare rather than to know the pride and the feeling of independence that comes with taking care of themselves. Entire communities in which everyone, every day, every hour, live in fear, for their personal safety - even for their, very lives. (Please understand, that I have no problem at all with welfare and food stamps and medical assistance when folks truly need it. That's what the rest of us are here for.)

What happened to mankind during this period between when I was a little boy growing up in my wonderful, caring, little town, and now? How did this terrible change come about? Is there anything that can be done to reverse it? Is there some magic formula you can use to make it all better – at least for you and the people near you?

I'll bet you expect me to say, "No, there is no magic formula that will make it all better." Well, surprise, surprise! That's not what you're going to hear, because I truly believe that there is a magic formula, and that my parent's generation knew it and practiced it, and as a result, created that wonderful, safe, loving, caring, place for me to live and grow and feel safe. Once you know that formula, I believe that you can create similar places for you and your children.

That magic formula begins with ideas about what's Fair and what's Unfair. When I was small, I'd often - and I mean many times each day - heard the adults around me use the phrase, "That certainly seems fair." These days, what is the phrase that we all hear and, perhaps, even use, instead? We hear, "It's just not fair." When was the last time you actually heard someone say, "That certainly seems fair." Maybe never? The world, in which fairness reigned supreme, has somehow become the World in which feelings of unfair just seem to be everywhere.

Let's talk a few minutes about this idea of fair. ... I don't believe that fair means I get everything I want to have. I don't think that fair means I get to do everything I want to do. I don't think that fair means life is always just great for me without my ever putting forth any effort to help make it that way. I do think fair means that I get most of those good things I'm willing to work for and therefore deserve, but, hold on here, I'm getting ahead of myself.

Most of us used to live according to an unwritten, even, an

unspoken, rule of life. I can't remember anyone even ever telling me about it in so many words. No one ever sat me down and said, "Tommy, here's the Rule of Life we all live by." We just all knew it was the way we were supposed to live together. Since it will be easier to discuss if it has a name, we can call this unwritten law, the Fairness Agreement. It went something like this: "I cannot expect people to do good things for me, if I am not willing to do good things for them." Let me say it once more before I explain it. "I cannot expect people to do good things for me, if I am not willing to do good things for them."

It says that it wouldn't be fair to just expect other people to take care of me or to give me what I need or want, and then let it just drop at that. It says that would be taking unfair advantage of other people and their generosity. It says that to be truly fair, there has to be a two-way give and take kind of relationship. When someone does something for me, I have to be willing to do something for him or to do something similar for someone else – often having even done it ahead of time. Anything else would be unfair, selfish, self-centered, greedy, dishonest, and not at all like the extraordinary human beings that we all can be. If we each believed that it was other peoples' responsibility to take care of us, then, there would be no one left to do the taking care of, would there? We'd just all be sitting around together, shivering and starving, waiting for someone else to come and provide for us. Instead, we have to share in the responsibilities of life - anything else wouldn't be fair - in fact, anything else could never work because the human species would have died off thousands of years ago.

Oh, we all know that there are a lot of hurtful, selfish folks in the World today, who will gladly steal from us or con us out of everything we have if they can, and then never feel so much as a twinge of guilt about it all. Usually, they even make it seem like it was all our own fault for being so weak as to let them take advantage of us. Worse still, many of us buy into that pile of garbage. Once we have been taken, we say, "Oh, it's my own fault, I shouldn't have let my guard down." Isn't it a sad and unfair state of affairs when we actually believe that it's ok for someone else to cheat us, to lie to us, or to steal from us, just because we let our guard down? Why should we have to have our guard up in the first place? If we all lived according to the Fairness Agreement there would be no need for guarding ourselves or our rights or our families or our possessions, would there?

I mentioned being human, a moment ago. I don't know how often you may think about it, but being a human being is a very special privilege - yes, I believe that *privilege* is the right word. Think about it. No other species, anywhere in the entire known universe, can solve problems like we can, learn like we can, love like we can, plan ahead like we can, decide to live in peace with one another like we can, trust each other like we can, or truly want to take care of each other, like we human beings can. I personally believe that when we find ourselves not living up to these wonderful, in-born, human possibilities, that we are actually no better than the lower animals - wolves, apes, toads. They live their lives according to the law of survival of the strongest, or take whatever you can, from whomever you can, as often as you can. Kill or be killed, seems to be the motto of the lower animals. Unhappily, that sounds a whole lot like the way millions of people are actually having to live today in the inner cities and, recently, even in many smaller towns – and more distantly in the so-called third world countries. There just seems to be nothing human to me about that way of life in which the meanest guy wins.

Why would anyone, why would you, for example, give up the chance to use your very special human skills, and just act like wolves and sharks and vultures, instead? It beats me, I'll tell you that for sure. Perhaps we have convinced ourselves that we have to act that way because those all around us are acting that way. Rubbish, my friend. Pure rubbish!! Let's never use that insanity as an excuse to sink down to their sub-human level of living. Let's never use that as an excuse to be anything less than this wonder-filled human being that you and I have this one, great chance to be.

Well, I got sidetracked there a bit. Excuse the sermon, if that's what it sounded like. It's just that I do so want your life and the lives of your children to be long, safe, and good ones - free from fear and pain and sorrow and misery and uncertainty, and, instead, to be safe, and filled with joy and happiness and caring and mutual respect.

Let me get back to how this Fairness Agreement works. When I talk with teens these days, one of their chief complaints about life and other people is that there is just too much unfairness in the World. If we want this World of ours to be fair, there is only one way it will ever happen. Let me say that again. If we want the World to be fair, there is only **one** way it will ever happen. And how's that? At all times, each of us must treat everyone else fairly. This is the magic potion! What could be simpler than that? Let me state it one more time. At all times, each of us must treat everyone fairly. That puts the first responsibility for a fair World, strictly on you and on me and on the kid next door and the old man down the street and the math teacher and your mom and dad and on down the ... well you get the idea. A Fair World doesn't just happen. Fair, is carefully built by you and me during every single day of our lives. That's the only way it can happen. That's what the history books tell us, and that's what common sense tells us. We all have to do our part to keep it alive and well. Anything less would be, should we say, *unfair*! In fact, we all really know that anything less just won't work. So, "I cannot expect people to do good things for me, if I am not willing to do good things for them."

Let me point out a few of the specific kinds of things that the Fairness Agreement requires of all of us who want to live in a World which is fair:

+   It says that if I want others to give me a fair deal, I agree to always give others a fair deal. Please note that this doesn't say: "You be fair with me first, then I'll be fair with you." It says that somebody has to start it all, and the only way for that to happen is if we all do it together. Once again, I cannot expect people to do good things for me, if I am not willing to do good things for them.

+   The Fairness Agreement also says that if I want to live without having to be in constant fear, then I never make anyone else feel afraid. Anything else would not be fair or human-like. Again, I don't wait around for them to prove their good intentions first. I don't say I'll stop terrorizing you once you stop terrorizing me. If we all said that, the terrorizing could never stop, could it?

+	It says that if I want to be able to always be safe, then I never do anything that will make things unsafe for others. Why? Because it is never fair to ask for something for myself, (in this case, being safe), that I am not also willing to grant to all others.

+	It says if I want to be able to trust what others tell me or promise me, then I never act in untrustworthy ways toward anyone else. It just wouldn't be fair.

The Fairness Agreement says much more than this. Later we'll talk more about it but these several examples should help you begin to see the fantastic kind of World that you can create when you don't expect people to do good things for you that you are not willing to also do for them.

Almost every culture in the World has this next, same, age-old saying that translates something like this: "What goes around, comes around." That sums up this fairness thing pretty well. It means that the way you behave toward others will eventually be the way others behave toward you. It means if you're a good guy other will be more likely to be good guys toward you. It also means if you're a bad guy bad thing will eventually catch up to you. It means when gang X kills a member of gang Y, then Y takes revenge and kills one from X, and then gang X in turn kills two more from Y, and on it goes forever. Or it can also mean, one of the guys with green skin does something nice for one of the guys with purple skin. Then, feeling kindly toward the green folks, the purple guy helps out two green guys and those two green guys help out four purple guys and ... well, again you get the point. What goes around, comes around.

Good or bad, what goes around comes around. So, we must each do our part to see to it that it is always only the good stuff that is going around! Sometimes good guys do get dumped on, but in the end, bad guys always do. Don't give up on the Fairness Agreement just because a few idiots refuse to see the light and choose to treat you poorly in response to your kindness toward them. Remember, you understand that the whole future of the human species depends on what you are doing so one or two or even two dozen bad experiences with the unthinking, uncaring, idiots of the World must not stand in your way from continuing to be one of the Good Guys. Helping to build a great future for all of the human beings who will ever live after you do, has to rate a thousand times more important than being a hurtful, selfish, take whatever you want, sub-human being today and tomorrow.

Fair means that there is always a cause and effect relationship going on. The only other choice to this Fairness Agreement is to live your entire life always being unhappy, afraid, on guard, and in constant danger. Does that surprise you?

Think about it. In those neighborhoods today where large numbers of folks don't live their lives according to the Fairness Agreement, life is terrible - possessions get stolen, property gets vandalized, no one feels safe, and even innocent little children get shot to death on their way to school. New businesses would never be so foolish as to move into such areas to provide the much-needed jobs that could help improve life there. Life gets so bad that young people will do anything to escape it - alcohol, drugs, and often, even more direct forms of suicide.

And what about those so-called bad guys who do get all of the stuff they want by just going out and forcibly taking it. Do they really ever find the good life they're after? Consider these things. In order to survive, the bad guys have to arm themselves with guns. They must restrict where they go and who they see or else put themselves in mortal danger. They have to live in constant fear of being killed or caught and generally do either end up in jail or done in by some rival. That just doesn't sound like the good life to me, does it to you? No one can possibly win in such a selfish society that tries to exist without the Fairness Agreement.

Almost everyone wins in a society that is based on the Fairness Agreement. Doesn't it make sense to try and rebuild your own little corner of the World in this way - in the image of how it used to be in my little town and can be again in yours? Maybe just rebuild your family first, or maybe just set up an agreement between you and one or two or ten of your best friends. Here's a mind-boggling fact for you to think about. If you made such a fairness pact with just two people, and they in turn each did the same with two others, and each of those four did the same, and so on, within just six months over two hundred million people could be a part of all this. The point is that we have to start somewhere. Don't we? We have to start with ourselves and the guy next door. Would it be fair to let this wondrous human species just destroy itself when we have such a powerful tool as the Fairness Agreement at hand to save it? The answer to that, my friend, now has to come from you and your generation. I hope you'll decide to make very good use of this magic potion I call the Fairness Agreement.

[Understand, you have to use common sense about your own safety and the safety of others as you pursue any approach to living.]

The Safe Technique

This section has nothing to do with sex - well, not directly, anyway - but still, I hope you will read it!

Another thing I frequently hear teenagers telling me these days is that lots of times it's really hard to know how to make the right choices when they are out with other kids. How can you know ahead of time whether doing something will end up getting you into trouble or just be fun? Most teens find that the S.A.F.E. Technique works pretty well.

The S.A.F.E. Technique is a quick check you can run on any situation. It takes around thirty seconds for you to complete and will help you decide whether or not what's about to happen is likely to cause trouble for you or your friends. It also can help you decide what you should do instead. Each letter in S.A.F.E. stands for one of four steps in this quick check-up technique.

'S' stands for STOP and SCORE the SITUATION. Stop and Score the Situation for possible trouble. You could simply call this using your brain and taking a moment to plan ahead. Think about what you are planning to do. If you have any doubt that it is not clearly *safe or right*, then immediately score it as possible trouble and stay away from it. Think about the very worst thing that might happen and then decide if that would mean trouble for you. Since you have no way of knowing ahead of time that that worst thing won't actually happen, get out of there as quickly as possible.

And don't let yourself get suckered into to playing the odds. This happens when you tell yourself things like: "Oh, there's only about one chance in ten that something could go wrong." That one chance in ten is more than enough to stop yourself right there. Here's why. Say that you do give into those one in ten odds on ten different occasions during a month. Since one in ten means just that, you can count on getting into big trouble on at least one of those ten occasions. So, if the odds are that there is any chance it could be trouble, just don't do it and you will be well on your way to staying out of trouble forever. Kids who keep getting into trouble usually don't understand how the odds work. Now that you do, you're way wiser than the average guy out there.

So, you say, that sounds good but how do I *not* go ahead and do it when the other guys are watching just ready to call me a wimp (or some other more colorful and humiliating four letter word). In fact, they might even hurt me if I refuse. Just hang with me here and a bit later I'll give you a surefire way out.

What if the thing that actually makes it seem exciting to me is that very chance that I might get into trouble - that I get a gigantic thrill out of living on the edge? Again, hang with me just a bit longer.

So, that is the "S" in SAFE. Stop, and Score the Situation for possible trouble.

Next, the "A" stands for ANALYZE. Analyze which of your needs would be met if you went ahead and did this activity, or went into this place, or whatever. Ask yourself, "What makes doing this thing seem interesting to me at this minute?" Often, it might seem to satisfy such needs as excitement, entertainment, flirting with danger, or perhaps a chance to prove you are brave, courageous, or skillful at something. It might seem like a way for you to get some money to buy something you want. It might meet your need to stay on the good side of your friends, to prove to them that you aren't afraid, or to simply keep from being bored out of your skull. For guys, it's often a way to attract or, at least impress, a girl.

All of these are all perfectly normal needs in people your

age - excitement, entertainment, flirting with danger, proving your courage or skill, living on the edge, attracting members of the opposite sex, making or keeping friends. You have every right to satisfy such needs and in the next step we'll talk about how you do that but here in step two, you are asked to just make a quick list of which of your needs might be satisfied by doing this questionable activity.

You can discover your needs by asking yourself, "If I do this, what will it get me, or how will I be better off, or why does it look like fun, or why do I think it will make me feel better?" Most kids who just keep getting into trouble never stop and think about why they need to do things, they just blindly (ignorantly) go ahead and do it and that *always*, eventually, leads to a person's downfall. Actually, it means those folks can't really be in control in of themselves, doesn't it?

So, in the second step of this SAFE Technique, A stands for Analyze your needs.

"F" stands for FIND (in this case!). Find other, safer ways for meeting those very same, normal needs that won't lead you into trouble. More trouble is something you really don't need, right! If it's your normal need for excitement that tempts you to do this dumb thing, then use your intelligence to think up some other, safer ways to experience excitement. If the need is to be accepted by your friends, then think about what kind of friends you really want to have - those who demand that you put yourself in danger, or those who are smart enough to help you find ways of having fun in safe and trouble-free ways.

It's always a good idea to have in mind a list or a menu of activities that will meet each one of your major needs - activities that are in line with what you believe about right and wrong, and that consider your safety and the safety of others. Then, when you feel the need for entertainment or for feeling powerful or for proving that you are charming, or attracting a certain boy or a girl, or whatever it may be, go to that mental menu to find a safe activity that will do just that! (Surely you are not going to tell me that you know yourself so poorly that you can't do that! Come now!!!)

> ❯   *Most often it's not the need that gets you into*

trouble, but the way you go about satisfying that need.

So, for each of your needs, I urge you to take time to write down a menu of things that you could enjoy doing that would not get you into trouble. This is how all trouble-proofed kids operate! It is how all trouble-prone kids don't operate. Don't cop out by saying there's no other way. Don't play dumb animal! You're a human being with a human brain and imagination. Use it! Practice using it until it works effectively for you in this very important area of your life.

But, back to this friend thing. What if there aren't any other safe guys in your neighborhood to be your friends? How do you just leave them and do without friends? I suppose this is the toughest question of your age. I know how important friends are to adolescents. I also know that nothing not even having friends is ever as important in the long run as protecting yourself against trouble. As we grow up and mature, we have to make many hard choices, and this is one of the earliest and undoubtedly one of the most important of them.

When you take time to see the long-term picture, it really isn't such a tough call. But I know it is so hard to see that big picture when it is you sitting there today, having to choose between trouble-prone friends or no friends. I suppose it comes down to this question, doesn't it: "Are you going to be in control of your own, safe, future and build it into a good one, or are you going to let those other kids make the dangerous choices for you?" Are you going to be like that empty beer can, just being swept along in the sewer, or are you going to take charge and steer your own course? No one, but a very mature you, can make that tough choice, right? I hope with all my heart that you're strong enough and wise enough to find a way to put your own bright future first. (How about only being with those trouble-prone friend inside your home? How about clubs at school – it could mean being with age-mates even if not your first choice of types. Is some safe alternative better than nothing?

So, "F" stands for FIND. Find other, safer ways for meeting those very normal needs of yours - ways that won't lead you into trouble.

The final letter, "E", stands for ESTEEM. In this case, Esteem simply means being able to feel proud of yourself - proud of yourself for obeying the rules of life that you have set for yourself. Self-esteem is the feeling one gets inside when he knows he has lived up to his own highest goals and the hopes he has for himself. Self-disgust or self-hate is the opposite.

So, after you have **S**cored the situation for possible trouble, **A**nalyzed why it seems attractive to you - that is, what needs it may be tempting - and after you use your activity menu to **F**ind another way to satisfy that same need, then you can **E**steem yourself. Respect yourself. Feel yourself just filled with SELF-ESTEEM, both because you were wise enough to keep out of trouble and because you were smart enough to find other ways to meet those normal needs and urges you had been feeling. Trouble-proofed kids do this, so you can, too. It's not that trouble-proofed kids are necessary any smarter than trouble-prone kids. **Trouble-proofed kids just always plan ahead better**. They always win in the long run. They use their intelligence in more sensible, wiser, ways.

Peer pressure? It doesn't really exist unless YOU let it!)

Now let's turn to a closely related topic; "PEER PRESSURE." I'm here to tell you, my young friends, that Peer Pressure does not have to exist for you! It never exists for trouble-proofed kids! ... How can that be? Let's begin with a story.

One Saturday night, not long ago, Jerry and Kyle were on the street corner talking with their friends and having a good time - just messing around – being normal teens. Bruce, the oldest and most influential one in the group, suggested that they break into old Mr. Stein's bakery and trash it. Mr. Stein had often run them out of his place in the past.

Without hesitating Kyle went along with the idea even though inside himself he knew it was wrong and understood that he could get into big trouble if caught. Also, without hesitating, Jerry said, "No thanks, guys. You're all going to be in big trouble and what you're thinking of doing just isn't right - it isn't fair to Mr. Stien." He immediately left the group, went home, and found another way to have fun. Kyle and the others were soon on probation. Bruce was in the Juvenile Detention Hall for six months. Mr. Stein went out of business because he couldn't afford to remodel the uninsured bakery after the boys vandalized it. Jerry, however, is living happily ever after!

Both Kyle and Jerry knew that vandalism was wrong. Still, Kyle went along with the group. Later, to the juvenile judge, Kyle blamed his actions on overpowering peer pressure that he just could not resist. Why was it peer pressure to Kyle and just a dumb idea to Jerry? Why did Kyle feel he had to go along, and Jerry didn't even give that a second thought?

Probably, because Kyle's good feelings about himself depended entirely on what his friends thought about him (externally directed). When they liked him he felt good about himself. When they disliked him, he felt bad about himself. Jerry's self-esteem, on the other hand, came from knowing deep down inside that he had done what he believed was right (internally directed). Kyle had never really known such a feeling of self-esteem. He had only known the fear of being rejected by others because there was no Kyle except as other people told him how he had to be.

Not long ago I heard a group of happy, well-adjusted teenagers, laugh out loud at the whole idea of peer pressure. I listened to them as they agreed that it's nothing more than a lame excuse made up by weak willed kids who don't have the guts to do what's right. More than that, however, I believe it's quite likely that some young people really aren't sure what is right. That's largely a matter of first having a set of positive beliefs and then just deciding to live according to them. Those beliefs are based on the Fairness Agreement, and I will discuss some of them a bit further along, here.

Have you ever wondered how you got the personality you have?

Let us think together about the four basic kinds of people in our World and how they each develop.

As we each grow older, we form ideas about what kind of person we believe we should be. How does this happen? It's no mystery, really. Although you don't remember it now, back during the first few years of your life you listened very carefully to what those around you had to say about you. You watched how they treated you and you paid close attention to what kind of feelings they produced inside of you. Then at some point around age four or so, you used all of that information (feelings you had and words you heard) to decide what kind of a person you were supposed to become. Of course, you didn't just sit down one day and say, "Ok, today's the day I decide what kind of person I'll be for the rest of my life". It all happened quite gradually and automatically way down in the deepest, most hidden, part of your mind.

If you heard these folks saying that you were a good kid, one who was loved and treasured, one they enjoyed having around, and you realized that they took very good care of you and handled you tenderly, then you probably got the idea you were a very precious person. You therefore probably became one of the good guys who now likes himself pretty well and in turn is one who takes good care of others.

If you were fortunate enough to have parents who expected you to follow the rules - not just once in a while but every single time - then you probably also grew up to be a pretty stable, mentally healthy, law abiding, and likeable person. (This doesn't mean that there may not have been times when you wished your parents would stuff those rules deep inside some disgusting bodily opening!).

On the other hand, if, during those early years, you heard things from your parents that made you believe you were no good, a bother, or of little value to them, or if you were ignored or often physically hurt by them, then you probably grew up believing that you must be one of the bad or at least unlovable, worthless, guys of the World. If the rules weren't regularly enforced, were changed without letting you know, or if your parents' reactions were impossible to predict, then you may have grown up pretty unhappy, less mentally healthy, and far less able to trust other people. All in all, just less able to cope even with life's more normal problems.

Happily, even such an unfortunate start in life as that, can usually be overcome if one is willing to take charge and really work at it. This ability to change and improve ourselves is one of those wonderful, in-born, features of this remarkable human species to which we belong. The problem is so common in fact, that there are several professions that do nothing except help folks learn how to overcome such unfortunate beginnings - counselors, psychologists, psychiatrists, certain social workers, and some clergymen – wise older friends, in fact.

In general, there are four basic kinds of personalities that develop from all those possible conditions I just listed. They each affect society in different ways. The first three of them tend to hurt us all.

Karri, for example, takes advantage of others, using people in whatever way fits her selfish purposes. She has no regard for the welfare of other people. If she thinks someone can help her get ahead, then she sticks with that person just long enough to get what she wants. Karri belongs to the personality type I refer to as the *People User*. The so-called suck-up or brown nose is another good example that we've all met and had to deal with.

Jim belongs to the *Observer* category. He is a person who just sits on the sidelines of life, watching it pass by without ever really jumping in and getting involved or making a difference in anybody's life. Observers like Jim don't have many friends. He'd rather watch a game than be a part of it. He'd rather read about romantic love than search for it himself. The Observer is just always on the fringe - always left out - and in the end is just forgotten. He hurts us all merely by not helping us – by not being a pleasant part of our lives.

Bruce is a good example of the third personality type - that of the *Destroyer*. He takes whatever he wants regardless of whom or what gets hurt in the process. Hitler was another destroyer. Mobsters are destroyers. Bullies, thieves, crooked politicians and drug dealers, are, like Bruce, all destroyers.

I'm sure it's clear to you that the Karri's, Jim's, and Bruce's of the World are never helpful to you or to me, or to society in general. In fact, each of them, in his own way, damages and destroys the good and fair way of life which most of the rest of us are trying to build and preserve. They do not follow the fairness agreement, do they?

The fourth category I call the Builder - the one who uses his or her special human talents to protect and improve society, our planet, and the lives of folks like you and me. The Builder understands the Fairness Agreement and uses it in all of his dealings with other people. Former president, Jimmy Carter is a good example of a Builder. So are Bill Cosby, Paul Newman, Jerry Lewis, Bono, Brad Pitt, Bill Gates, and Ellen DeGeneres. All of them give tirelessly of themselves and their money to make life better for other human beings. (You can name others).)

Unlike all other animals in the entire known universe, we humans have this built-in capacity to be Builders. Because of that, I think it is our duty - our obligation - to each try and become a Builder. Only the Builders can protect and improve man's chances at living the good life, free from fear and poverty, sickness, and unhappiness. I think we both agree that it seems very important that we do just that. I hope that you will take time to discover and develop your own special talents in order to become all that you can become as a human being – a Builder. To do any less lets you, and all of us, down. Humans should take seriously their responsibility to live up to their impressive human possibilities.

All youngsters who get into trouble over and over again fall into one of those first three hurtful personality categories. They are either a People User, like Karri, an Observer, like Jim, or a Destroyer, like Bruce, or, they are some combination of the three. Virtually no kid who is constantly in trouble ever comes from the Builder category family. On the other hand, all trouble-proofed kids - that is kids who are able to keep themselves out of trouble - are members of the Builder category. So are about 95 percent of their parents, by the way.

It is hard to stress strongly enough how important it is to model ourselves after the lives and beliefs of the Builders. Since Builders live by the Fairness Agreement, they just automatically do helpful things that make life and living pleasanter, easier, and safer, for all of us. Builders realize how precious this human species is. Builders strive to protect us all, to care for us, to improve us, and to help us each reach our greatest potential. Not to become a builder, I believe, is to admit that one is totally satisfied to just live his life like a savage or the other beasts of the animal kingdom.

You might enjoy reading the books I have written about *The Little People of the Ozarks* - tiny, helpful, magical beings that spend their lives being helpful to us humans when we need outside assistance. The books are fun, and they demonstrate how Builders go about living their lives, and show what a fine World they can build. You might also enjoy my book, *Ripples* about how the lives of a runaway teenage boy and an old man come together to change each other for the better.

Problems vs. troubles! They are NOT the same.

At this point, it seems important for me to point out the difference between having a life free from *problems* and having a life free from *troubles*. Life is always going to be filled with problems. Some will be big ones. Most will be small ones. Problems are things such as not earning enough money, not finding the kind of friends we want, not having clean socks, not getting along at work or school, having a really bad hair day, breaking a fingernail, having the car breakdown, getting dumped by a girlfriend or boyfriend. But problems can usually be solved or at least handled without any terrible, long lasting, bad effects. In fact, though you may not have realized it, without having problems to solve human beings begin to lose their ability to think and to be creative. So, we all need to have at least a few problems just to keep going and growing. Its like necessary exercise to keep our mind's in good shape.

By trouble, on the other hand, I mean really serious situations that a person got himself into because he misbehaved, or broke a law, or went against some other major rule of society. A problem might make you unhappy for a short time until you solve it but trouble can get you punished in a big way – for the rest of your life in some cases. It can land you in jail, cause you to become disowned by your family, get you beat to a pulp, or something worse. So, I am not promising that you will never have any problems if you live according to the suggestions in this manual. I am promising that you will know how to keep yourself out of trouble FOREVER, and be a happier, more likeable person, who will truly love himself, will find that in the long run others really like him, and will be filled with great gobs of self-confidence.

Basic Values

Let me return to the concept of *fairness* for just one more moment because it is such an important belief - a belief without which mankind will, without any doubt, kill itself off during the next dozen decades.

Many of the inner-city teens I talk with these days - teens who have grown up in the worst of slums - have developed a very different way of defining this term, "fair." Jeremy, for example, put it to me this way: "You see, when I finally get all the same stuff that the rich kids have - then things is fair. When I got all that stuff, then that means everything is right. When I don't got all that same stuff, that means things ain't right - that things is wrong and unfair."

Like Jeremy, most of these money-poor teenagers truly feel that life owes them the very same good things and pleasures that the richer kids have. And, since life owes it to them, you see, it is then ok to just go out and take what they want from whomever has it. This kind of out and out stealing is in no way wrong to them. In fact, since life owes it to them, it is the only right thing to do. WOW ! ! ! In other words, in order to make life fair for themselves they have the unquestionable right to be unfair to the rest of us.

Now, if someone then steals that very same stuff from them, that, they believe, is unfair. As Jeremy again told me: "THAT kind of a thief deserves to be killed, 'cause it's always wrong for anybody to take my stuff. I'll kill 'em if they trys it". Double WOW!! Of course, this way of defining "fair" is actually the exact opposite of the Fairness Agreement, isn't it! It says, "I can take whatever I want, because life owes it to me, but nobody else ever has the right to take my stuff."

Many of the younger teens who have never known any other meaning for the term, "fair," really can't understand why the rich folks and the cops think that's wrong. I hear them saying things like: "They just don't understand how it is." "If they can't protect their stuff, they shouldn't get all bent out of shape when I take it, you know!"

I'm fascinated by their idea that "life" owes it to them. What do they mean, "Life owes it to them?" It seems they believe that just because they are alive, they deserve to have a good life. Well, if you have come this far in this chapter, you know that I won't disagree with them on that idea. I too believe that just because we are alive as this magnificent human being we each do deserve the best possible life. You deserve it. I deserve it. The old man across the street deserves it.

Those kids and I do, however, disagree in two major ways. First, we disagree about how this good life should come about, that is, how they should obtain that good life. Second, we disagree about what that good life really is. They say it's having lots of stuff like the rich kids have. I say it has nothing to do with stuff but more about that in a minute. I suppose there is also a Third way in which we disagree. I believe it is important for us to protect the human race from being destroyed and they, quite clearly, could care less about the human race as a species, right?

I've talked a lot about my idea of "fair," and how it is never right to take from others if we aren't also willing to give to them. That makes it pretty clear that I would disagree about stealing, doesn't it. Once we steal something we always - day in and day out - have to live with the fear that the person we stole it from (or the police) will hunt us down and punish us. That just doesn't seem like a very smart way to go about building a comfortable, safe, and happy life for yourself. Would you agree?

I have a suggestion for you to consider. I suggest that it is only fair that we must all earn what we get. We save for it, we trade other possessions or services for it, or we find a way to create it for ourselves. In poor areas this may seem impossible to the young folks and for a few, it may be. If they weren't trying to base their happiness on having stuff, however, being rich or poor really wouldn't have to matter because stuff wouldn't matter so much.

What can be more important than stuff? I'll get to that pretty soon and first I'll ask you to think about this. In every single neighborhood, regardless of how poor or crowded or crime infested it may be, there are always a few young people who find ways to beat the odds. They find ways to succeed in honest ways that don't hurt anybody. They find ways to climb out of that neighborhood and rise above the problems there. What do they know that all the others don't know? I believe it is very simple. It is the beliefs they hold about what is truly important in life - about what is right and what is wrong, what is fair and what is unfair, and about what it really takes to be happy.

Let's take a brief side trip, here. Remember with me if you will the names of all those successful celebrities, actors, rock stars, whomever - the ones who seemed to have all the money, stuff and fame one person could ever want – and yet were still so terribly unhappy that they killed themselves. Who would be on your list? Mine contains: Marilyn Monroe, Janis Joplin, River Phoenix, Kurt Cobain, Cory Monteith, and even a nice, bright kid from a rich family just down the street from me. Did having all that money, stuff, and fame make them happy? Obviously, it did not. In fact, do you know what group of people in our country goes to psychiatrists and psychologists the most? It's the rich and the famous - about twenty times as often as the rest of us. That may be partly because they can more easily afford such help, but the bottom line is that even with all of their money, stuff, power and fame, they are still so unhappy that they need professional mental health counseling in order to go on with their lives.

So, does money and stuff automatically make one happy? I hope that you understand it does not. This doesn't mean that stuff and money can't be enjoyable, because it can - remember, I know about such things. I was one of those rich guys once. That gave me the chance to discover firsthand that wealth had nothing to do with my deep-down inner happiness - the only happiness that lasts and really counts, by the way. During the past several years I got rid of all that money and stuff. I am now as happy as I have ever been, living, I am told, below the poverty level.

I am not telling you that you shouldn't want an average standard of living. I am not telling you that having certain things

won't bring you a really nice kind of momentary pleasure. It may.
A stereo, a car, clothes, and trips to wonderful places are all great.
What I am saying is that if you count on those things - all that stuff
- to bring you *basic, forever and ever,* human happiness, you are
on the road to a very sad and gloomy life, just brimming over with
disappointments, frustration, and dissatisfaction.

Before I tell you my secret to happiness - that is, what it is
that is really more important than stuff - let's explore the whole
idea in another way. Using that excellent, bright, open mind you
possess as a fellow human being, think about the following three
situations.

You are riding in an elevator. There are two complete
strangers riding with you - a man and a six-year-old girl. Suddenly
the man stops the elevator, pulls a gun, and, pointing it at the little
girl says to you, "If you don't give me all your money and your
watch, I'll kill her." What do you do? Which is more important to
you the life of that young stranger or your stuff?

Here is a second situation to think about. You have one
thousand dollars in your bank account that you have been saving
for a car. One day you get the chance to attend a two-week
survival course out in the wilds of Colorado. It will be a chance to
see what you are made of - a chance to prove to yourself that you
have what it takes to make it on your own, something you have
often wondered about. It costs seven hundred dollars. Do you go
and put yourself to the test or do you save the money for the car?

Here is a third example. A friend of yours comes down with
leukemia - cancer of his blood. He has to have a bone marrow
transplant in order to have any chance to live. It costs two hundred
and fifty thousand dollars, which the family does not have. His
mother comes to you and asks if you can contribute something to
help him. What do you do with the thousand dollars in your bank
account? Buy the car or help your friend?

In each of those situations, which outcome was more
important to you? Was it your stuff and money or was it your
feelings about yourself and others - your beliefs about what was
the right thing to do? If, in all three cases, it was stuff and money
that won out, it is no surprise to you by now to learn that you are

not at this time one of the Builders of the World. So, the rest of us humans must understand that we cannot count on you to help us survive, to improve ourselves, or better the condition of humanity in general. If, however, it was your feeling - your belief about charity, compassion, and self-knowledge - that was more important, then, you just proved an important point about yourself. When it comes right down to it, stuff, is not as important to you as knowing deep down inside you that you have done the right thing - the fair thing - the thing that proves you are easily able to display your very special human side. Congratulations, my friend, you are a Builder.

After saving the little girl's life, after trying to help save the sick friend's life, after proving yourself out in the wild, you could go to bed at night and feel pleased with yourself. You could say, "I did the right thing today and I am so proud of myself." It is a wonderful feeling, knowing without any doubt that you are one of the good guys, one of the Builders, one of those who subscribe to the Fairness Agreement - a totally and forever trouble-proofed person.

How would you have felt if the little girl had been killed but you had been able to keep your watch and money? How would you feel, never having been able to find out for yourself if you would have been strong enough to really have survived that wilderness experience - you'll never know of course if you didn't try? How would you feel if you hadn't contributed to your friend's medical fund and he had died? Even if he had died after you had contributed, you could have at least said, "I did all that I could have done so I'm pleased with myself for that."

Let's try a less extreme example, a more everyday type of example. Say that it is early evening as you walk down the sidewalk on your way to a party. You pass a very sad looking old lady. At that moment you have a choice, don't you? You can speak to her and try to brighten her life a little bit or you can ignore her and hurry on, so you won't be late to your party. Now, slip ahead and see yourself in bed that night thinking back on the day. How will you feel about yourself if you know you just ignored her - making no attempt to let her know that there were really nice, helpful young people out there in her World? Did the stuff - in this case getting to the party on time - make you feel happier inside than if you had stopped to help? How would you feel if you had stopped and taken those thirty seconds or sixty seconds or even five minutes to say something like: "Hi! A beautiful evening isn't it! Hope you'll be able to enjoy it! By the way, I'll be happy to help you cross this busy intersection if you want me to? I don't mean to be pushy but I'd sure be happy to." How would you feel as you lay there in bed remembering her smile and her feeble "Thank you," as she patted your hand and looked gratefully into your eyes - perhaps a single tear making its way down her timeworn cheek?

Nine beliefs held by most Builders

Well, there are Builders and there are non-builders. I hope you can find a way to remain or become a Builder. There are several basic beliefs that most Builders share. I'm going to talk very briefly about nine of them. See if they make sense to you. If they do, I suggest that you re-read this section later and copy them down so you can review them every once in a while - well, every morning would be best. That's how I have done it for the last forty-some years. It gets me off to the right start. It gives me that Builder's set for the day. It reminds me who I want to be. It's worth a whole lot more to me and to those I will meet that day than an extra two minutes of sack time would be.

The First belief is; I cannot ask anyone else to do helpful things for me if I am not also willing to do helpful things for him or for someone else. This is really the Fairness Agreement that we have already discussed. It is a key trait of the Builder Personality, and is the exact opposite from the People User, the Observer and the Destroyer.

Second, as a Builder I believe that I have the right to keep my life for as long as it naturally lasts. In most situations, I must grant all others this same right to keep their lives for as long as they naturally last. In other words, if I want you to let me live, I must agree to let you live.

A Third belief is this: As I was growing up, I needed the help of many other people along the way, so now, I have to be willing to help this new group of kids as they also grow and search after their way. The Builder remembers about and appreciates the things freely done for him by other people - people such as parents, neighbors, farmers, friends, teachers, policemen, soldiers, perhaps clergymen, even those who (way in the past) built the sidewalks and the streets he uses and the building in which he lives. They all helped me, so now, being the older one, it's my turn – my opportunity – to do the helping.

Fourth: Since I need to be able to trust those around me, I, myself, must act in trustworthy ways toward everybody else. Builders are trustworthy and they trust other people until they prove they can't be trusted. If we all waited around for the other guys to first prove they are trustworthy, no one would ever take that first step and we would just remain a human species of untrusting, fearful, sorrowful, beings.

Fifth, the Builder understands that in order to be a happy, well-adjusted, person, I need to receive approval from others, and I must therefore also give approval to them. None of the three hurtful personalities can ever know or understand the wonder-filled feeling of having won someone else's sincere words of approval. It may come in the form of a compliment, a pat on the back, a word of praise, a satisfactory school grade, a raise for outstanding performance on the job, or some other form of deserved congratulations. These things help us feel great about ourselves. The opposite of all this is the put-down. Builders never seriously put-down others. People who put others down are usually only trying to make themselves look better without having to really ever do anything that actually makes them better. Put downs are the lazy man's way to self-esteem (of course it is a fully false and undeserved sense of self-esteem).

Sixth: In order to be a happy, well-adjusted, person, I need a few good friends, so I must also be a good friend to a few other people. There is an old saying, "You must *be* a friend to *have* a friend." It's often true. People aren't likely to try and be friends with someone who never seems to try and act friendly toward them. Builders act friendly and therefore make many good and dependable friends.

Seventh: Helping those around me stay happy will

increase my chances for a happy life. Nothing can ruin your life faster than having to be around somebody who is never happy - always angry or sad or plays the know-it-all. So, doing what you can to make them happier people will usually make your own life a whole lot happier as well. The opposite is also true, of course. When you make those around you sad or angry, it spills over into how they treat you and makes your life miserable as well. Revenge can *only* make things worse because it makes others dislike you more and it makes them less happy people. The popular saying, "Don't get mad, get even," is a perfectly terrible suggestion for how to go about solving problems and how to apply the fairness agreement. Getting even always creates new problems - the other person then tries to get even with you for what you just did, and then you, again have to try and get even with him and so on for a hurtful, sorrow-filled lifetime.

Eighth: Since positive strokes and tenderness are needed for happiness and good adjustment, I will regularly give positive strokes and show tenderness to those around me. As just stated, the Builder understands that living among unhappy, maladjusted people is *always* uncomfortable, so helping them become better adjusted and thereby making everyone's life more pleasant, only makes good sense. It is usually quite simple to accomplish. Be tender rather than rough with them. Make them feel comfortable when they are around you. Do this by building them up and never tearing them down. Let them know what things about them you appreciate or admire.

And finally, *the Ninth belief: Being this marvelous human being that I am, I have the right and duty to become a Builder.* Builders believe they should discover their own special abilities, talents and skills, and then work to develop them. They believe that they should also help others work to improve themselves.

I am certain that by now you understand where I think humanity and this precious World of ours will end up if, generation after generation, we continue to produce People Users, Destroyers and Observers instead of Builders. The best route to becoming a truly trouble-proofed person is to be raised by parents who are Builders, and who go out of their way to help their children learn and accept the Builder's philosophy and the Builder's approach to defining, finding, and living the good life. When one's parents aren't Builders, then the teenager must try to take charge of his own philosophy and beliefs about fair and about right and wrong behavior and live his or her life as close to those ideals as possible.

Jay:
A young man who turned his troubled life around!

Now, I want you to meet the very special young man who I introduced to you earlier. During our time together I considered him a close and precious friend. He is one who has had to take this second route - to take charge of his own philosophy and beliefs about right and wrong, and begin building a new life for himself, all quite separate from his original family. Jay, welcome to my book.

Jay: I'm happy to be here, Tom. Thanks for inviting me to be part of this.

TG: Jay, we've known each other for how long now?

Jay: I'd say it must be pretty close to a year.

TG: Gee, it seems like a lifetime, my friend. Life hasn't been easy for you, or always kind to you, has it?

Jay: No, but it's been what it's been, and that's that. You move on. The bad stuff is all mostly in the past, now. Sometimes it almost seems like a dream - a bad dream, I suppose.

TG: But it's a bad dream that you're learning to put behind you. So many of the young people I know who have been through similar experiences, just can't seem to do that - to see it as a bad dream - now mostly over - and get on with life. You are accomplishing this though, and we all want to learn your secret, if there is one. I think it will be most useful if you would begin your story backwards, Jay. Tell us about yourself as you are today. Then, we'll take a look at where you used to be - where you have come from

Jay: Ok. Well, I'm seventeen and I am on my own. I'm living independent from my family. That gives me a lot of freedom but also a lot of responsibilities, too. I have my own apartment that I had to furnish. Now I have to pay all the bills myself - gas, electricity, phone, cable, rent, food, clothes - everything is my responsibility now. I saved up and bought a used truck. That takes gas and very expensive insurance. Let's see, what else. I have a job as a cook in a restaurant. I started out as a dishwasher about a year ago and just worked my way up to cook. It doesn't pay a lot but it's a good job for now. I have a lot of good friends where I work. I had to give up all of my old friends - they were all bad news - drugs, drinking, trouble with the law. It's not easy to find new friends when you have a rep like mine. I do have a wonderful girlfriend and we help each other. She was just like me only she had other problems, too.

TG: And most important of all, perhaps, Jay, is what?

Jay: Sobriety!

TG: Tell us what you mean by sobriety?

Jay: No drugs. No alcohol ever again. You see I'm an alcoholic and a drug addict, so there is only one way back for me - just never even think about using again.

TG: How has sobriety changed your life?

Jay: Well, in a lot of ways. I have my life and I probably wouldn't if I'd kept going the way I was going. For another thing, I'm able to begin thinking about my future. I never used to be able to take my future seriously because I didn't think I had one - and I was right, back then, I didn't have a future.

TG: Ok. Now that we know the Jay of today, go ahead, and start way back at the beginning. Tell our friends the brief edition of your story.

Jay: I only lived with both parents a short time before they got divorced. Dad had problems taking family responsibility and mom used drugs and drank for as long as I can remember. My older brother and I were on our own since I was real young. My own Dad first gave me drugs to use. Can you believe that? My own Dad! Since then, I've used everything there is. I've popped all the pills, smoked all the weeds, shot up with everything imaginable. I was in dozens of different schools and dropped out for good way before high school. I hated school and teachers. Out of all my teachers, only one was special because she'd listen to me. I didn't have her long. My mom fixed me up with sex for my first time - with one of her friends. I was about twelve, I guess. One good thing though, I had to learn about working at an early age. I'm sure that has helped me a lot. I've lived in dozens and dozens of places - too many to count. About eighteen months ago I hit rock bottom and was forced into treatment. It was the best thing that ever happened to me - that and then my job at the restaurant where all the grown-ups helped me so much.

TG: Jay, you're a young man of great courage and we all appreciate your willingness to share your story with us. As I listened to you just now, I kept asking myself this question. "What is there about Jay that has made him able to stay completely away from alcohol, drugs and trouble, and get on with this new life of his?" As I said, so many young people I've known, Jay, seem to get off to a great start in treatment - just like you did - but then they soon find themselves falling back into their same old, deadly ways. What's different, what's special, what's unique about you and your situation, Jay?

JAY: I've wondered a lot about that, too. I suppose it's a couple of things. As I remember it, I was really a nice little kid, so I must have had something going right, way back then. I just really can't remember about that time - I was so young and my brain got so messed up along the way. I think I knew my Mom and Dad loved me even if they didn't have a clue about how to be good parents and to raise – as you put it – trouble-proofed kids.

And I was always curious about everything. I was always asking questions and trying to find out how things worked and what people thought about things. I wanted answers!

TG: That sounds like a real strength to me. If a youngster isn't curious enough to ask the right questions, he can't ever get the right answers, can he?

JAY: No, he can't. The trouble is I started asking my questions to the wrong kind of people, so I got the wrong kind of answers.

TG: What do you mean the wrong kind of people?

JAY: Out on the street where I lived, all there was, was other losers, you know. Maybe they were older and more experienced, but they had no way to know the best - the right - answers about life and things like that. Growing up stuff.

TG: In other words, the kind of people who would have had the best answers to your questions about life just weren't available to you back then. But, being a curious boy, you still asked those questions and sometimes you received pretty poor answers.

JAY: Right! But now, since treatment, all that's different. Oh, I could still hang out with the wrong crowd. I always have that choice. But now I have the choice to have the right crowd in my life. The old crowd just drug me down with them. The new one helps me out - it makes me think about better ways to do stuff and to think about things. I think that's what I always wanted. It's sure what I always needed, anyway. That's what all kids need. Good models, I think you'd call them.

TG: And during the past several months you've certainly become a good model, yourself, Jay. One of the other things I see that is different about you is that, now, at least, you spend a lot of time thinking about how you are going to build your own future. The losers who I've known have just never seemed to be able to get started down that track.

JAY: They give up when they don't see all the good changes happen right away and they think all the changes they do make should be seen right away by everybody else. That just doesn't happen. It all takes time. I think those kids you're talking about are too impatient about it all. I mean, sure, I want to have a good life and have fun right now, too, but I know I have to do the kinds of things for fun that won't get in the way of that good life that I want to be living tomorrow and next year and when I'm old like you - no offense. It's like you said in the SAFE check-up, I have to find ways to meet my needs and desires that won't get me, or my girlfriend, into trouble.

TG: You're saying that staying out of trouble requires some planning ahead of time.

JAY: Yeah, it does!!! Lots of planning ahead! You always have to be asking yourself, "What does it get you?" "What does it get you in the long run?"

TG: That's a big order for teenagers who are not usually known for their patience or ability to look way ahead.

JAY: I suppose so, but that's what adolescence is all about, right - growing up and learning how to be more patient and beginning to live in the real world instead of the make-believe world we all lived in when we were little kids. When you get shot in the real world, you just can't get up and keep on playing. Most likely, you're dead.

TG: You hit the nail on the head, there, Jay. Adolescence is that time when we need to leave the fantasies of childhood behind. We can't all be movie or rock stars, or the best looking or the most talented, or the smartest, or the richest, or the most powerful. We all have to discover what we have going for ourselves as people and use that as the basis to build our lives.

Back toward the beginning of our chat, Jay, you spoke of how you learned about the value of working when you were still quite young.

JAY: Yeah, I mowed lawns and had a paper route, and handed out flyers - anything to make money.

TG: And what do you think all of that taught you that you might not have learned any other way?

JAY: Well, for one thing, it kept my time filled so I didn't have time to be bored and didn't need to go looking for something - anything, really - just to keep me from being bored. The other thing is that when you work you have less free time, and that makes it more valuable to you when you do get it, so you make better use of it I think. Another thing, when you have a job it's earning you money and you don't want to take the chance of losing that job by getting yourself into trouble during that free time or doing stuff that will make you late to work - because if you're late, your fired.

One thing I'd like to suggest to kids who have a hard time staying out of trouble, is this: Fill up your time with good things. Like, get a job, join a gym or a Boy's Club, or help out with little league or something like that. It's just plain dumb to let yourself be bored because I think that always leads to trouble.

TG: That's great advice, Jay. Kids, who fill their time doing schoolwork and other organized activities, are many times less likely to get into trouble than are those who don't keep busy in those ways. Sports, jobs, clubs, gyms, scouts, and volunteer work are all great ideas. But how about being more specific, now, about what else you believe working taught you.

JAY: That work equals freedom, and that gives you self-respect.

TG: Work equals freedom and that gives you self-respect. Explain that for us.

JAY: Well, when you work you get paid, right. And when you have your own money you don't have to depend on anybody else for stuff, so you have freedom. And when you have freedom that means you can take care of yourself, get what you need, and get what you want - and when you can do that, you can respect yourself.

TG: Over the years I've heard hundreds of kids moan and groan about having to work, but you're saying that learning, early in life, about what went into being a good worker, actually helped you out.   That it made it easier for you to become this more responsible person in the long run.

JAY: It sure did. And working's a lot different from just going out and stealing. I've stolen stuff before, lots and lots of stuff, and sure, it was nice having it, but stealing it never gave me any of the good feelings about myself that I need in order to respect myself. And if I can't respect myself my life really isn't worth much. And when life doesn't seem like it's worth living, then you don't have any reason to take care of yourself, so using drugs and drinking and having unprotected sex is no big deal - It just doesn't matter. You don't care if it kills you, or if it takes control of your life, or fries your brain, because you just don't care when you can't respect yourself. Sometimes I think I even hoped some of that might kill me. No, I'm sure I did.

TG: Both of us have known lots of kids who fit that description, haven't we?

JAY: We sure have. I was one, you know.

TG: Isn't it great to be able to say "was one," instead of, "I am one, or, every day having to ask the question, "Am I one?"

JAY: It sure is. The question really is: "Do I want to be where I was before, just thinking about this minute, or do I want to reach for the really good stuff that can last forever."

TG: That brings to mind another closely related topic. Reputation – I believe you used the shortened term, rep. Here you are, telling the World about your past. Aren't you afraid that your reputation as an undesirable person will follow you if you let us know all about it this way?

JAY: Because of all this stuff I've been through, I've learned one really important thing about a rep – reputation. "Usually, you're not to blame for who you've been in the past, but you sure are responsible for who you are from today on."

TG: So, you're saying that what you used to be is just that - what you used to be - but who you are today and who you become tomorrow, is what's really important.

JAY: Yeah, I'm working hard at building a new reputation for myself, and I have to ask my new friends to let me start over - to just let the past be the past and accept me for who I am today. Then I have to come through and prove it.

TG: Well, as I hope you know, Jay, you've convinced me, and many, many others as well. Do you have any last advice for our friends who will be reading this?

JAY: I'd say that to have self-respect is about the most important thing there is in life. Without it, there's just no way to be happy. In order to have self-respect you have to know what you believe is right and wrong for yourself and for all people in general. I mean, you can't just think of your own needs. You also have to think about what other people need and what they have a right to have. And then, always try to do what you think is right for everybody. Never be ashamed to stand up for what you think is the right way to live. Never be ashamed to show others that you are that good kind of person. And never give in to those who try to drag you away from your good beliefs about yourself, and about other people, and about the good way you want to live your life.

TG: Thank you so much, Jay. I can't think of any more powerful way to end this chapter than that.

* * *

It is my sincere hope that what has been said here will stimulate each reader to take control of his own life, and begin building that wonderful, trouble proofed life, based on trust, helpfulness and self-respect, that is your highest calling as a fellow human being.

[More >]

Parting Remarks

All people are precious. When we haven't learned this as children, living is far more difficult than it needs to be both for us and for others. Interacting positively and helpfully with our fellow human beings is the single most important social goal we can pursue. Not doing so, condemns one to a trouble-prone life. Seeking out the actual facts and basic knowledge related to the problems and tasks that confront us makes us strong, contributing, dependable people. Relying on opinion and folklore (street talk) makes us dangerous to ourselves and all others.

Mastering the well-established principles for raising happy, mentally healthy, children is absolutely essential to anyone planning to be, or who finds themselves being, a parent. The only reliable method for raising a trouble-proofed child involves helping him or her learn a positive, socially responsible, set of personal values, such as those based on the eight tenets presented earlier. Knowledge about how the human mind works and how it accepts and rejects information and direction is a necessary part of being an adequate, effective person. We must each understand our normal human needs and devise ways to satisfy them all in socially acceptable, non-hurtful, ways. The only useful approach to problems is to be appropriately armed with the real facts and problem-solving techniques, and never rely on merely worrying, getting angry, or giving up.

Learn and apply these principles and you will be a happier and more self-fulfilled person yourself, better able to raise trouble-proofed children. In the process, you will be passing on to all future generations of human beings those beliefs and skills necessary for the continuation of a happy, healthy, growing, and caring, human race.